on track ...

Bob Seger

every album, every song

John Van der Kiste

SONICBOND

sonicbondpublishing.com

Sonicbond Publishing Limited
www.sonicbondpublishing.co.uk
Email: info@sonicbondpublishing.co.uk

First Published in the United Kingdom 2026
First Published in the United States 2026

British Library Cataloguing in Publication Data:
A Catalogue record for this book is available from the British Library

ISBN 978-1-78952-651-6

Typeset in ITC Garamond Std & ITC Avant Garde Gothic
Printed and bound in England

Graphic design and typesetting: Full Moon Media

on track ...

Bob Seger

every album, every song

John Van der Kiste

SONICBOND

sonicbondpublishing.com

Acknowledgements

My thanks are due to Kev Hunter for supplying some excellent images and material from his collection of vintage music papers, to Elizabeth Kane and Les McStrachan from the Frankie Miller Respected! Facebook page for their help, and to Gareth Colgan for his keen interest when we corresponded online on the subject. As always, I am indebted to my wife, Kim, for her support during my writing and research. Last but not least, thanks to my publisher, Stephen Lambe, Dominic Sanderson and the rest of the editorial team at Sonicbond.

on track ...

Bob Seger

Contents

Author's Note

All songs described in the text are credited to Bob Seger alone as a writer unless stated otherwise. US chart positions are from *Billboard*; UK chart positions are from Official Charts. Three of the 1960s singles (by Bob Seger and The Last Heard, then The Bob Seger System) reached the *Cash Box* top 100 and another four the top 200, but only two of these, both by The System, entered the *Billboard* top 100. All release dates are US.

All albums were released on Capitol unless stated otherwise. The three albums credited solely to Seger on Reprise between 1972 and 1974 were the first to be issued in the UK at around the same time as on Palladium in the US. Of the earlier titles, only *Ramblin' Gamblin' Man* and *Mongrel* were in Britain, several years late. UK release dates of albums from 1975 onwards were generally about two weeks later than in the US.

Certification figures are US unless stated otherwise. Due to declining sales of physical music in the streaming era, recent albums have not yet attained certification status, and probably never will.

The Early Years

From the late 1940s, Detroit was renowned for its thriving eclectic music scene. Although recognized primarily as the city that gave birth to Tamla Motown, it was also home to various blues, jazz, rock and soul artists. Many of them spent some time building a reputation on the local scene before breaking out nationwide across the United States and then further afield. One such act was Bob Seger, who paid his dues with a band on the live circuit and made records for several years, becoming a local hero long before breaking big across the nation.

Robert Clark Seger was born in Detroit on 6 May 1945, the second of two sons. His father, Stewart, was a medical technician with Ford and General Motors, and played clarinet, guitar and piano. The younger boy learned a good deal through listening and watching him play. When he was four, he started singing, his first favorite tune being 'I'm Looking Over A Four-Leaf Clover'. By the age of ten, he was playing his father's bass ukulele and teaching himself chords from a book he was given. This happy childhood ended when the hard-drinking Stewart, whose marriage had become increasingly stormy, left his wife, Charlotte, and the boys, George and Bob.

The family struggled financially for several years, and Bob increasingly turned to his radio and guitar. When he was 15, he and two fellow schoolmates at Ann Arbor High, Pete Stanger on guitar and R. B. Hunter on drums, formed The Decibels, with himself on vocals, guitar and keyboards. Their main musical influences were Little Richard, whose vocals made him a role model for the teenage Bob, Elvis Presley and Buddy Holly. Seger wrote his first complete song, 'The Lonely One', a year later. It was one of three songs they recorded, another being George and Ira Gershwin's 'Summertime', at a studio owned by Del Shannon, with Del's keyboard player, Max Cronk (best remembered for playing the musitron in the instrumental break on 'Runaway') supervising them. About half a dozen acetates of 'The Lonely One' were pressed, and it was played once on a local radio station. The band played local gigs at weekends, while Bob helped to provide for the family by following in his father's footsteps, working briefly at Ford and General, then in a clothing shop by day, and as a pizza deliveryman by night.

By 1964, the national music scene had been transformed by a combination of the 'British invasion', spearheaded by The Beatles' and The Rolling Stones' first American tours, and the burgeoning popularity of the major Motown and Stax performers and of soul singers such as James Brown, Solomon Burke and Wilson Pickett. Seger loved all these as well as contemporary singer-songwriters, with Tom Rush being a favorite. Several bands were formed in and around Detroit, the most significant being Mitch Ryder and The Detroit Wheels, with their fusion of soul and rock, and Motor City Five, later MC5. It was a diverse mix of styles that left its mark on the young singer, from rock 'n' roll and blue-eyed soul to folk and acoustic.

Bands formed, split and morphed regularly into other bands. By 1964, Seger had joined The Town Criers on lead vocals, plus John Flis on bass, Pep Perrine on drums and Larry Mason on lead guitar. A few months later, he joined the better-established Doug Brown and The Omens. Seger and Brown shared vocals, and the former recalled that they were opposites in several ways. As a big fan of James Brown, whose *Live At The Apollo* album was, at the time, his favorite album, he was 'the R&B guy in the band', the soul man, while Doug Brown and the others modelled themselves more on The Beatles and The Rolling Stones. Doing up to five sets a night, six days a week, he said later in Brian McCollum's 'A Definitive Oral History Of Seger's Early Years' article in the *Detroit Free Press*, 'You can sing just about anything, your voice gets so developed, so I developed a really wide range. I could do all the falsettos.' Seger and Brown were signed by Shannon as songwriters to his publishing company, Shidel Music, and recorded at least one demo with Shannon on backing vocals.

Soon after he joined, around the end of 1965, the group released their first single, 'TGIF (Thank Goodness It's Friday'), written by Brown, with Seger on vocals. Early the following year, they released a novelty item, under the alias of The Beach Bums, as a double A-side, the only record on the Are You Kidding Me? label. The one that gained the most attention was 'The Ballad Of The Yellow Berets'. Credited to 'D. Dodger', it was a parody of the patriotic single by Sgt Barry Sadler, 'The Ballad Of The Green Berets', which spent five weeks at number one in the US and reached number 24 in the UK. The 'Yellow Berets' lyrics suggested that they were taunting draft dodgers with cowardice, although some thought it was ironic and was really a protest, anti-war song. Sgt Sadler was not amused, and a 'cease and desist' order halted further distribution and airplay.

By now, Seger was beginning to write his own songs as well as sing them, and word spread that he had talent in this direction as well. Glenn Frey, a future founding member of the Eagles, became a friend at about this time and looked up to him as a kind of older brother, acknowledging Seger as the first figure on the Detroit rock scene who was doing his own material. They spent a good deal of time together, much of it driving around listening to records on the radio and discussing what they liked or didn't like. If Frey didn't want to hear something and tried to push the button to find another station, Seger told him to stop and listen, reminding him, 'They're on the radio; we're not.' On another occasion, Frey told him that he would never get anywhere unless he wrote his own material. 'What if they're really bad?' Seger asked. 'Well, the first few probably will be bad,' was the reply, 'just throw those away until you write a good one' (quoted in the 'Seger's Early Years' article).

Around this time, Seger met the man who would become his manager and co-produce many of his records with him. Edward 'Punch' Andrews was a local musical entrepreneur who had launched his own small independent label, Hideout Records, and with his business partner Dave Leone, ran a few local clubs that regularly put on live bands. Leone, Seger, Brown and Dave Whitehouse co-wrote 'Get Down On Your Knees', a single by The Underdogs, the band fronted by Whitehouse as lead vocalist. They were also offered one of the first songs Seger wrote on his own, 'East Side Story', but he was unsatisfied with their version, and decided he could do it better himself.

He and Brown had decided to go their separate ways, and he formed another band, which he named Bob Seger and The Last Heard. Accompanying him as vocalist, guitarist and keyboard player were Carl Lagassa on guitar, Dan Honaker on bass and Bob Evans on drums, replaced after the first single by Pep Perrine. Andrews signed them to Cameo-Parkway Records, and 'East Side Story' became the first of five singles released by the label. All were local hits in Michigan, though none made the national charts. The following year, Seger wrote, produced and arranged both sides of the only single, 'Miss You' and 'My Boy', by all-girl quartet Mama Cats. Two of them, Laura Polkinghorne (later Creamer) and Joan Sliwin, would later appear as backing vocalists on his albums from the early 1980s onwards. He was also involved in the only 45 made by Glenn Frey's band The Mushrooms, writing, producing and arranging 'Such A Lovely Child' and its B-side 'Burned'.

Throughout a career spanning more than half a century, Andrews would be Seger's right-hand man, a relationship of mutual trust that would give the latter a degree of stability that most other musical performers could only dream of. When he was on the verge of retirement, he told journalist Steven Wheeler in an interview that their time span of working together as artist and manager must be a world record, like a long marriage in which they fought and rejoiced in equal measure.

> The way it works is that I mainly maintain the creative end, and when we have problems, it's usually when he gets too involved in the creative side. And we also have problems when I get too involved in the business end [laughs].

Bob Seger & The Last Heard

'East Side Story' 2:25 b/w **'East Side Sound' (instrumental)** 2:25

Released on Hideout in June 1966 [A-side credited to Bob Seger on label, B-side no artist credit]; reissued on Cameo-Parkway in October 1966 [both sides with full singer and band name credit]

The song, regarded as Seger's first single proper, was by any standards an impressive debut. A burst of percussion is joined by fuzz guitar and a booming bass riff, leading into a song of one night of teenage lust between Johnny Brown and his sweetheart. He insists that he has to leave, despite her begging him to stay with her and not go uptown with his knife. In the last verse, there's a knock on the door from two men arriving with bad news. So much for the story. The vocals are identifiably the 21-year-old Seger, joined on the chorus by the others in what sounds like a nod to Van Morrison's 'Gloria', originally the B-side to Them's first hit, 'Baby Please Don't Go'. Just before the verse comes a wild organ break, and the sound is reminiscent of early Doors (think of the guitar throughout 'Hello I Love You'), who were recording their first album at around this time. The instruments create a similar storm on the B-side.

In an interview with Roy Trakin of *Creem*, 20 years later, Seger admitted that he 'might have been a little derivative at that point' because he didn't think it would be 'his song'. He recalled losing some sleep over the fact that 'it sounded an awful lot like 'Gloria', though if you put them side by side, they're not really all that alike. There are a lot more chords in 'East Side Story' than there are in 'Gloria'.'

A clip featuring the band performing 'East Side Story' on what is presumably his debut TV performance can still be found online.

'Sock It To Me Santa' (Seger, Honaker, Lagassa, Leone) 2:13 b/w **'Florida Time'** (Andrews) 2:10

Released on Cameo-Parkway in November 1966

Everyone involved undoubtedly had some laughs in the studio putting this raucous but enjoyable little festive novelty together. 'Christmas won't be a drag, Santa's got a brand new bag', they sing to a fast-paced 12-bar blues-styled song that pays homage to James Brown and Mitch Ryder. Listen carefully: when they're not singing, 'Sock it to me Santa, just bring me a sled', they throw in a few seconds of 'Deck the halls with boughs of holly'. The B-side, 'Florida Time', credited to 'Punch' as writer, had served the same role on the other side of 'Ballad Of The Yellow Berets', although it was not credited to The Beach Bums this time. After listening to its cheery, sun-soaked vocal harmonies and organ, it's evident that they could have made a good living as a Beach Boys tribute act as well.

'Santa' was almost forgotten for many years, but eventually received a new lease of life on two various artists festive compilation CDs. The first was *A Rock 'N' Roll Christmas* (Polygram Special Markets, 1994), which bundled it together with ten other Christmas tunes from Bon Jovi, Chuck Berry, Elton John, The Kinks, Billy Squier and The Moody Blues, among others. It was followed by *Little Steven's Underground Garage Presents Christmas A-Go-Go* (Wicked Cool Records, 2008) as one of 20 tracks, a selection also including Wizzard (non-charting unknowns in the US), The E Street Band with Darlene Love, The Brian Setzer Orchestra, Clarence Carter, The Ramones, Keith Richards and Rufus Thomas. Wicked Cool Records was a garage rock label founded by Steve van Zandt of The E Street Band, who ran a weekly syndicated radio show and was keen to bring what he considered were some unjustly overlooked yuletide records to a wider American audience.

'Persecution Smith' 3:02 b/w **'Chain Smokin''** 2:43
Released on Cameo-Parkway in February 1967
In this satirical narrative, which takes a shot at half-hearted revolutionaries, Persecution Smith is here, there and everywhere, uptown and underground, on every protest. There's an arresting guitar intro, and the vocal is spoken rather than sung; more than anything else, it brings to mind 'Subterranean Homesick Blues' and 'Bob Dylan's 115th Dream' from Dylan's fifth album in its quickfire lyrical content, if not quite so breathless. The B-side is a throwaway novelty song, in the tradition of old 1940s and 1950s country tunes like 'Smoke! Smoke! Smoke! That Cigarette' and 'Chew Tobacco Rag', which were regarded as quite acceptable in an age when smoking was more prevalent and did not carry the same stigma as it does today.

'Vagrant Winter' 2:19 b/w **'Very Few'** 2:30
Released on Cameo-Parkway in April 1967
This was an odd song to release at the start of summer, with its imaginative if unseasonal references to vagrant wintertime, and December's children, who learned to live without the sky as they huddled by the fireside. It's lighter in tone than most of the other singles, and quite catchy despite the somber lyrics, with its garage rock organ reminiscent of the band's labelmates, Question Mark and the Mysterians, and their sole major hit '96 Tears'. The B-side sounds utterly unlike anything else the band ever recorded, a pretty love song out of the 1940s that would have been perfect for the likes of Bing Crosby.

'Heavy Music Pt 1' 2:32 b/w **'Heavy Music Pt 2'** 2:32
Released on Cameo-Parkway in July 1967
'Heavy Music' is one of those astonishingly simple numbers that defies analysis. Basically, it's one of those dance numbers of the time where everything falls into place – riffs on bass, piano and guitar, drums and handclaps, with the title chanted ad infinitum, a few basic lyrics about listening to the radio when the big bad beat comes on and having a good time. Dave Whitehouse, maybe other members of The Underdogs and possibly Glenn Frey joined in on backing vocals. It's safe to assume that the

band were more or less jamming, and as the tape rolled, they ad-libbed a few lyrics as they went along, including 'Stevie Winwood got nothin' on me' near the end of Pt 2. (Around 1991, Seger said in an interview that he had recently seen Winwood on TV and was astonished to hear him still singing, hitting the high notes like he was 16, adding that he wished he had a voice like that.) It amused Seger when some listeners tried to find a sexual innuendo in the phrase 'goin' deeper'.

Such petty controversy was not enough for radio stations to consider banning it, and the general reaction was so good that it hit pole position on the Detroit charts, reached number 82 in Canada and was on the verge of the Billboard top 100 (number 103 in the 'bubbling under' chart) when Cameo-Parkway's business problems eclipsed them and the company was closed down in September 1967. When fans complained that they couldn't obtain the record, Seger visited the offices to ask why, and found the place was empty except for a janitor who was cleaning up the premises. Later that year, the label was acquired by entrepreneur Allen Klein, later manager of The Beatles and The Rolling Stones, and renamed ABKCO, but all sales momentum had been lost.

'Heavy Music' had also been issued as a single in France (on Stateside), Germany (on Ariola) and Japan (on Cameo, through Victor Records). ABKCO would reissue a selection of their singles in the US only from acts including The Rolling Stones, Herman's Hermits, Chubby Checker and Bobby Rydell between 1972 and 1975. Among them were Bob Seger and The Last Heard's 'East Side Story', 'Persecution Smith' and 'Heavy Music' in 1972, and 'Heavy Music' again in 1974, suggesting that there was still some residual demand.

A compilation album containing both sides of all five of Bob Seger and The Last Heard's singles, *Heavy Music: The Complete Cameo Recordings 1966 To 1967*, was released on CD and vinyl by ABKCO in 2018, the first time they had been available in any form since Cameo-Parkway ceased to exist.

The Bob Seger System

The band were continually proving a good live draw, and beginning to get exposure on TV and local radio, although it was suggested that having a name like 'The Last Heard', obviously chosen as a joke, was easily '*mis*heard' on radio when DJs played the records on air, and not calculated to help airplay. A new era would dawn with a change of name. Lagassa left, Bob Schulz was recruited on organ and they became The Bob Seger System.

Andrews' search for a new deal with a major label led to several rejections. At length, he approached Tom Gelardi, promotions manager at Capitol Records, who set up a showcase gig at a small club for the band, which would be attended by his Head of Artist & Repertoire, Carl Engelman. After hearing a few songs, Engelman told Gelardi that Seger was an outstanding writer, and he was very keen to have them. He was not alone. Motown, which was about to sign white pop and rock acts like Rare Earth, R. Dean Taylor and, a little later, British singer Kiki Dee, was also in the frame and offered more money, but for various reasons, Seger and Andrews preferred the idea of joining an organization that already had The Beatles and The Beach Boys. A contract was signed, and the band continued to work the live circuit while recording a single, followed by their debut album.

'2 + 2 = ?' 2:45 b/w **'Death Row'** 2:53
Released in March 1968
Both tracks of the single appeared on the first and second albums, the A-side being slightly different on each. See album reviews below for descriptions.

Ramblin' Gamblin' Man (1969)

Personnel:
Bob Seger: lead vocals, guitar, piano, organ
Dan Honaker: vocals, bass
Pep Perrine: backing vocals, drums
Bob Schultz: organ
Michael Erlewine: harp
Glenn Frey: backing vocals, acoustic guitar
Penny Lawyer: backing vocals
Produced by The Bob Seger System and Punch Andrews
Release date: April 1969
Highest chart positions: UK: NR, US: 62
Running time: 36:07

According to Seger's brief note on the back of the sleeve, 'The title of this album up until three days ago was 'Tales Of Lucy Blue'. At that time, I realized that Lucy Blue is Ramblin' Gamblin' Man. Thank you, Dr Fine!' This was Richard Fineman, a Capitol executive, who decided at the last minute that it would have greater appeal if renamed after the track that had already been a top 20 entry. The original artwork was based largely on the central figure from Botticelli's painting *The Birth Of Venus*, but Capitol decided that a design directly inspired by Renaissance art was at odds with the marketing strategy for the genre of music they and the band were promoting, and could have an adverse impact on sales. A new illustration, depicting a mysterious-looking woman in an art dress on what looks like an icy Arctic shore, proved a satisfactory compromise.

Following in the wake of a national hit (also released in the UK but without charting), the album was a minor success that summer, selling enough to give the Capitol management some faith in their new signing for the future. Their plan was to try to build up national success at home before trying the British and international markets. This was a long time coming, and didn't happen until the label had dropped them, signed them again and at last saw them achieve significant mileage. It was belatedly released in the UK in 1977, and again in 1981 on EMI's mid-price Greenlight label. With more live dates, including some on which they opened for The Beach Boys, and occasional TV appearances, their reputation continued to grow, but for the most part, they remained local heroes while meaning very little to the wider public beyond.

'Ramblin' Gamblin' Man' 2:20
The infectious opening track, and the song that gave Seger his first hit, it was released as a single in October 1968 and peaked at number 17. They had always loved The Spencer Davis Group's 'Gimme Some Lovin'', featuring Steve Winwood's insistent Hammond organ riff, and he asked Schultz to play

something that would suggest that feel but without copying it. The organ dominates over the infectious riff, a three-chord sequence that never deviates from E, D and A, with the pulsating drums and bass adding fire. Glenn Frey was credited with vocals and guitar, joining in on the call and response routine on the chorus line, although his contribution on the instrument is all but inaudible.

In the lyrics, Seger sings of a boy who left home at the age of 13 and has been on the move ever since. He's like 'The Wanderer' in Ernie Maresca's hit about a Jack the Lad who proudly leads a devil-may-care existence. He's a drifter, so don't get attached to him, as he will only leave you with a broken heart. There's an endearing roughness to the sound that radiates atmosphere, reminiscent of the style of contemporaries such as Mitch Ryder & The Detroit Wheels, and it wouldn't sound out of place on a Northern soul compilation album. As Don Henley, Frey's fellow Eagle in future years, would later approvingly tell the singer, 'It's not really all that great a song, but your voice makes it sound like a great song.'

Original American promo copies credited Bob Seger alone on the label, as did stock pressings in France and Germany on the label and picture sleeve. Black Oak Arkansas released a more guitar-driven version in 1976 on the album *Great Balls*, and as a single in the UK.

'Tales Of Lucy Blue' 2:23

This was intended as the album's title track, and also as the A-side of the single, until radio DJs rightly decided that 'Ramblin' Gamblin' Man' was the more commercial of the two. Seger lets rip with a heartfelt vocal about a mysterious lady with a 'piercing smile filling her face for a little while', who seemingly remains just out of the reach of her admirers. In contrast to the intensity of his singing, his menacing yet restrained lead guitar, Honaker's chugging bass and a steady beat on the drums and cymbal play it cool.

'Ivory' 2:25

With a dash of Motown and a bluesy shuffle, shimmering organ and insistent bass throughout, not to mention a snarling guitar solo on top, this has a touch of Rolling Stones misogyny in the lyrics. The woman who's the subject of the song, we learn, was born with a face that would let her get her way, and had everything she wanted – a theme Seger would revisit in 'Hollywood Nights'. Again, his vocal sounds like he's about to catch fire. The second single from the album, it scraped into the chart for one week at number 97.

'Gone' (Honaker) 3:25

There could hardly be more of a difference between this and the three preceding numbers. Bassist Dan Honaker takes lead vocal on a gentle, largely acoustic song that's reminiscent of Tim Hardin or Tom Rush. There's a slightly hippy, trippy air of unreality that matches the lyrics about a girl who pulls up a chair to sit by the gravestone of her departed lover, 'remembering his eyes when she lied, knowing she lives, feeling she's died'. The verses feature his voice on its own, a contrast with the chorus's rich harmonies and echoing distortion.

'Down Home' 3:10

Back to R&B, and a gritty number that has Seger wailing over what's basically a 12-bar blues in disguise, with Honaker adding occasional vocals mixed well back. The tone is set from the word go by Erlewine's wailing blues harp, before bass, guitar and drums kick in, and there's a fadeout and brief return in the final minute. The lyric is a cheerful series of mini-sagas about three rather eccentric characters, suggesting a nod to Dylan's 'Highway 61 Revisited'. Erlewine found the harp work quite exacting, as Seger had insisted on his playing in the unusual key of F sharp, not a natural one for the harmonica. 'There were two keys I could blow, and he wasn't willing to modify it even half a step', he commented. 'That will tell you a lot about him and the way he worked.'

'Train Man' 4:05

More than any other track on the album, this shows the shape of things to come within a few years. A folk ballad, opening softly with acoustic guitar and piano, this paints a picture of love gone wrong in the tale of the 'train man' who comes in the night, having touched a girl's heart, taken it apart and then gone. Seger sings softly at first, but around halfway through hits the high notes, while a guitar solo adds some fire. This was a style that would find its ultimate realization in 'Night Moves' and similar numbers in the same vein.

'White Wall' 5:15

The two longest tracks follow, both hitting five minutes plus. The lyrics of 'White Wall' are about the loss of innocence and disillusion that maturity brings, once the 'springtime of your years' is over. It's a dreamy, eerie number, with the vocals mixed well back before it gives way to a murky-sounding jam that descends into distortion, reminiscent of what Pink Floyd were doing at the time.

'Black Eyed Girl' 6:30

This sounds like nothing so much as Seger's attempt to unleash his inner Jimi Hendrix. If so, it doesn't really work. It's a rather formless song, probably improvised in the studio while the tapes were rolling, about an old flame who was 'a little bit wild but all right', and whom he once saw with another man (echoes of 'Hey Joe'?). It is surrounded by some riffing on guitar and bass while the drums gently hold everything together. It sounds fairly spontaneous, again with vocals low in the mix, and sounds like it could well have gone on much longer than six minutes. And Seger's soloing fails to catch fire in the way that Jimi Hendrix's generally did, although admittedly the latter's style was hard to beat.

'2 + 2 = ?' 2:47

Although the debut single never charted, the A-side has long since been regarded as one of the most powerful anti-war songs of its time, alongside Creedence Clearwater's equally angry 'Fortunate Son', released about 18 months later. This obviously gave a truer indication of Seger's stance on the Vietnam conflict than The Beach Bums' 'Ballad Of The Yellow Berets'. Seger sings softly at first before his voice erupts in anger. He questions the validity of the war from the viewpoint of a schoolboy being drafted to serve, railing about the fate of a friend buried all too soon in the mud of a foreign jungle land, having 'died to save your lies'. All this is set to an opening bass riff that's echoed by lead guitar, with drums supplying a steady backbeat, while the backing vocal chants 'Two plus two is on my mind'.

On the single, about 20 seconds before the end, everything is momentarily interrupted by a loud, distorted guitar chord, which then disappears as the vocals and other instruments continue until the fade. This is absent from the album version, where the backing vocal chant continues uninterrupted until the fade. It was thought to have been added as AM radio stations took exception to the momentary silence at that point.

'Doctor Fine' 1:05

There's little to be said about this fragment, which could have been taped while they were warming up in the studio, added as filler and named after Fineman for want of any better ideas. It's just one minute of a bass riff, joined by drums and then organ (presumably played by Seger, as he had the writing credit), that comes and swiftly goes.

'The Last Song (Who Needs To Be Loved)' 3:02

This was the age of hippie songs, of 'make love not war', that spawned singalong anthems like 'Everybody Get Together' and later 'Give Peace a Chance'. One short verse along the theme of 'Don't you know it doesn't matter who you are or what you'd really like to be' flows smoothly into a communal chorus of a whole crowd, or repeated overdubs from the band, of 'Love needs to be loved'. Perhaps 'Hey Jude' was an inspiration as well. It may be slight, but charming in its way, and a pleasing conclusion to an album that encompasses a fair range of styles.

Noah (1969)

Personnel:
Bob Seger: lead vocals, guitar
Tom Neme: lead vocals, lead and rhythm guitars, piano
Dan Honaker: backing vocals, bass
Bob Schultz: backing vocals, organ, saxophone
Pep Perrine: drums, percussion
Produced by Punch Andrews
Recorded at GM Studios, East Detroit
Release date: September 1969
Highest chart positions: UK: NR, US: -
Running time: 34:25

Despite some chart success for their first single and album, this was the start of a difficult time for Seger. Schultz left The System on the eve of a national tour, and as there was no time to find and rehearse a replacement, they were reduced to a trio with their frontman having to handle organ as well as vocals and guitar.

In order to ease the strain on him when they were obliged to record another album straight afterwards, Capitol and Andrews between them recruited a new guitarist and keyboard player, Tom Neme, to collaborate on writing new material, while Schulz rejoined. The result was a quickly-recorded ten-track album set with five songs credited entirely to Neme, just one to Seger and a couple of collaborations with Honaker and Perrine, plus one from Honaker alone. According to a note on the back of the sleeve:

> The first album was trio, this album is more in many respects. It's more sound, it's more guts, it's more soul and it's more conflict. Conflict between two very different types of music. Side one is Bob Seger – moody, dynamic, human. Side two is influenced by Tom Neme, a new and important addition to The System. It is this influence that is creating change. Seger will always be Bob Seger; any change must come from The System and Tom Neme.

Noah has always remained Seger's joker in the pack, the odd one out in his discography. Although it is his face alone on the front of the sleeve, unlike the other two System albums, it's the only one that can't be called a Bob Seger record through and through. When his 'worst to best' lists are compiled, it invariably ends up at the bottom. True, it has its defenders (or apologists?), and it's certainly not unlistenable except for the fifth track, but over half a century later, it remains more of a curiosity than anything else.

Even a cursory listen suggests that his heart was simply not in it. Maybe he was being made to feel that he was seen as an inadequate frontman who had to be sidelined or at least needed a colleague who could have been his equal. It's noticeable that he collaborated as a writer on only two numbers on the whole album, 'Innervenus Eyes' and 'Cat' (which can hardly be called a song), and these with the other members, not with Neme. He only wrote two songs on his own, one of which was an old cut from earlier sessions. The newcomer had a McCartney-esque gift for melody, but on the whole, his style was more lightweight, and it's an uneasy balance between his material and Seger's generally more Lennon-like, hard-hitting approach, which is far less in evidence here than on the first album. If Capitol and Andrews thought that adding him to the lineup would help them to create an American version of The Beatles, they were sorely mistaken.

'Noah' 2:57

Seger never came closer to pure pop than with the album's title track, a likeable, infectious, if slightly cheesy, singalong tune, driven along by piano and acoustic guitar. Replace the former with organ, and it might almost be The 1910 Fruitgum Co. of 'Simon Says' fame. The lyrics, addressed to a certain Noah, are the simplest of rhymes, verging on bubblegum; one verse goes 'Hoist up your sail, Go kill a whale, Don't look so pale, Noah'. Musically, the verses are based around two chords, and the sax break on just three chords. Catchy it may be, though number 114 would be its chart peak as a single.

'Innervenus Eyes' (Seger, Perrine, Honaker) 2:42

Back to hard rock meets soul fusion, as Seger sings, or rather declaims James Brown-style, of a woman who's 'looking so good'. The simple but effective riffing on fuzzed-up guitar and organ, and a tantalizingly brief guitar break, followed by a section where everything but the drums cuts out behind his urgent, almost screamed vocal, keeps the energy factor at fever pitch throughout. It was the album's second single in the US, but it didn't chart.

'Lonely Man' (Neme) 3:09

On Tom's first composition to grace this album, there's a good song struggling to get out. To Seger's vocal, the writer adds a call-and-response routine, and the guitar work is quite catchy. But it's let down by one frightful moment in the lyrics department. Anybody prepared to commit lines like 'Oh, I wish that I could find me a ducky/Yeah, got the urge to go quack quack, yeah/Then I know in my heart I would be lucky' to vinyl must be having a laugh.

'Loneliness Is A Feeling' (Neme) 3:05

The mid-tempo first verse on this tale of love gone wrong is powered by shimmering organ, with a strong accent on the drums, then giving way to a more restrained section where gentle guitar takes over, reverting to the first verse pattern with the title repeated over and over again. It's pleasant enough, but rather unadventurous, and gives the impression that it could have been developed further.

'Cat' (Seger, Perrine, Honaker) 6:20
Now for something completely different – or should that be unlistenable? The longest track by a fair margin, and arguably Seger's worst ever, comprises over six minutes of funky metallic percussion. There's nothing else to it but muffled, grunted vocals consisting mainly of somebody groaning as he enjoys himself under the sheets, punctuated by shouts that call to mind a half-hearted imitation of 'Sympathy For The Devil'. You hardly need to hear this more than once. At least Neme, who is uncredited on the label and sleeve with this noise, was blameless.

'Jumpin' Humpin' Hip Hypocrite' (Neme) 3:07
As noted on the sleeve, Seger had sung lead vocal on the first five tracks, and Neme did likewise on the next four. This play on words introduces an energetic, quite funky song about a live wire, another Jumpin' Jack Flash-type character perhaps, who's always on the move and can't sit still. The bubbling guitar and organ hold it together, and it's one of the more commercial tracks that might have been a potential single.

'Follow The Children' (Neme) 3:09
Another catchy, rather sweet, if very untypical, song that could have been a hit. With a prominent jaunty piano, it has an optimistic lyric about watching children playing in the sand and 'building a rainbow to fantasy land'. Its message is 'the reason for living is just to be free', a chant that is repeated gospel-style on the fade.

'Lennie Johnson' (Honaker) 3:01
'Here we go, tape rolling Sergeant Pepper, take six', an engineer calls out teasingly at the start. This one sounds very much like The Beatles or Idle Race in their most psychedelic moments, a song about an oddball character who's lost his way, and with an attractive George Harrison-style guitar break towards the end.

'Paint Them A Picture Jane' (Neme) 4:03
This time, Neme seems to be heading for Crosby, Stills & Nash territory. On the whole, it sounds passable, if a tad sugary, despite a moment of darkness in the line 'If they ask you why I'm crying, Just tell them someone is dying'. The build-up towards the end with harmony vocals and organ is the best part.

'Death Row' 2:52
After a clutch of enjoyable, if rather too sweet, songs, the closing track brings us back to earth with a bang. They certainly saved the best till last, and

some regard this and 'Innervenus Eyes' as the album's only saving graces. An outtake from the ***Ramblin' Gamblin' Man*** sessions, this started life as the B-side of '2 + 2 = ?'. It puts much of the rest of the album in the shade. Just under three minutes of pounding garage rock, a cavernous-sounding guitar swathed in echo provides a backdrop to the desperate song of a 21-year-old prisoner on Death Row. Although the title is absent from the lyrics, it's clear what the song is about. The prisoner sings of passing what remaining time he has left smoking and drinking coffee, every minute seeming like five, as he braces himself for the countdown to the electric chair.

Mongrel (1970)

Personnel:
Bob Seger: lead vocals, guitar
Dan Honaker: vocals, bass
Bob Schultz: backing vocals, organ, saxophone
Pep Perrine: drums, percussion
Produced by The Bob Seger System and Punch Andrews
Recorded at GM Studios, East Detroit
Release date: August 1970
Highest chart positions: UK: NR, US: 171
Running time: 33:44

Recording *Noah* was and would always remain the lowest point of Seger's career. He was so disappointed with it and with the label's apparent intentions regarding Neme that he seriously thought about leaving the music business altogether. It was as if he had lost confidence in himself. A mismatched, not to say inferior talent, had been foisted on them and dominated proceedings. Exhausted and disillusioned, he disbanded The System and enrolled in college.

Fortunately, there would be a happy ending. After Seger retired completely from music half a century later, he explained to Steven Wheeler that the suits at Capitol wanted the band to be more democratic and less of a one-man band. They intended him to write and sing fewer of the songs himself and allow the others more of a chance. As he was under contract to those who called the shots, he did so but reluctantly, and a lackluster album was the result. Neme, he was told, was being hired as an extra guitarist, and then took him by surprise when he came up with several songs that he wanted them to do. It was as if he wanted to become co-leader, if not outright frontman. He admitted he didn't really like Neme's songs, and more importantly, felt they were wrong for the band. 'It was like the Eagles hiring Barry Manilow,' he laughed, 'and then six weeks later [Capitol] were telling me, 'I think we made a mistake."' Two driving forces trying to pull the band in different directions didn't work.

What he called his 'retirement' lasted a few weeks, and it gave him a chance to review his future. To everyone's relief, he reformed the band without Neme, who left the rock industry and found a new calling in Christian music. No longer overshadowed by someone with ideas apparently above his station, he felt rejuvenated, and it was back to business.

Although in control again, he still felt he was under pressure. They were playing so many shows, often two a night, that he didn't have enough time to come up with new songs, and really 'had to write on the run.' In spite of this, the sabbatical had evidently not harmed his career. The band attracted an ever-growing following with more and more gigs, as well as completing a third album. The result was what many regard as Seger's hardest rocking platter ever, despite the very un-rock 'n' roll sleeve design. It shows a 19th-century painting by an unknown artist of a small girl and her dog facing each other over a table. Seger saw it in a restaurant in East Detroit and immediately decided he wanted it as it would fit the record perfectly.

In *Rolling Stone*, January 1971, Ben Edmonds gave *Mongrel* a positive, if not wholly uncritical, review. He found it 'easily Seger's best work to date, but there are still some crucial musical problems he must come to grips with if he is to realize the tremendous potential he displayed on his earlier Cameo-Parkway singles (most notably 'Heavy Music' and 'Persecution Smith').' While he praised the singer for writing 'marvelous rock 'n' roll songs in the virile 1965 mold, somewhat of a lost art these days', he thought the band itself was rather like hard rock contemporaries Mountain, who had become something of a byword for excess, and the record 'often degenerates into 'heavy' overstatements of the most clichéd sort.' Long-term fans who are familiar with Seger's earlier catalogue also generally regard this as his finest achievement so far, the one where he really found his voice as well as his songwriting muscles.

It was first released in the UK in 1977, and again about five years later on EMI's mid-price label Fame.

'Song To Rufus' 2:44

If the half-hearted *Noah* failed to catch fire, then Seger was revitalized by feeling back in the driving seat. He seized the reins on its successor and amply made up for it from the very start. With a single beat of the drums, 'Song To Rufus' hits the ground running. Neither the organ nor the guitar stray far from a single note on each chord, but sometimes simplicity works best as his vocal cords sound fit to burst on this relentless boogie shuffle, singing about leaving on a Delta plane to Atlanta – 'I'm a junk runner honey, hotter than the noonday sun'.

'Evil Edna' 3:11

After that explosive start, it's a pause for breath on a more mid-tempo song. Seger sounds more restrained, but can still allow himself the occasional controlled scream as he sings about a femme fatale, the mysterious Edna, who 'looked just like a gypsy'. The music is just as intriguing as the lyric, culminating in a solid wall of sound from what sounds like an organ and a guitar played through a Leslie speaker that comes to a sudden halt at the end.

'Highway Child' 2:49

Another ferocious rocker, this has something of a Bo Diddley trademark shuffle, even a nod to the sound that Motörhead would capture some years later in all its rawness, albeit at a more breathless pace, on 'Ace Of Spades'. Seger growls and howls, the organ and drums provide a brisk rhythm and the guitar solo manages to sound melodic and wild at the same time.

'Big River' 3:10

Although Seger was known as a full-tilt rocker, the inner singer-songwriter in him that was bursting to get out made its first appearance on this lovely song. He desperately wanted to write a few slower numbers, he explained. The problem, he said, 'was that it was very difficult for my bands to play anything with any kind of sensitivity or delicacy. They were always big bashers, and every time I'd write a ballad, they just bash it to death.' Much as he loved to rock, it was important to have balance as a songwriter. It was something that he'd learnt from The Beatles in particular: 'They could rock really hard and they could also do ballads and cover both ends, and that's what I wanted to do.'

This one, fortunately, was granted some 'sensitivity'. A number with piano as well as guitar to the fore, a few discreet chimes and some gorgeous vocal harmonies, its lyrics liken life to a big river. He allows himself some more philosophical reflections, advising his audience in the final verse, 'Follow your heart, follow your rainbow, and you're gonna find you are not alone'.

There would always be a close association between Seger, Glenn Frey and the latter's band, the Eagles, who would form about a year after the release of this album. As a thank-you to Seger for his friendship and encouragement, though they never released it (a recording is said to exist somewhere in the vaults), they would include this song in their early shows. No less importantly, in style, it's a forerunner of his wistful, more restrained songs like 'Night Moves'.

'Mongrel' 2:20

After that peaceful interlude, back to the rock. Piano, organ and drums bubble ferociously, while the guitar screams on a song about a 'mongrel with the hard sell'. Some might hear an echo of this in the Deep Purple classic 'Black Night', which would follow on the other side of the Atlantic within a few months.

'Lucifer' 2:26

Lucifer spends his days ramblin', gamblin', livin', shovin', well aware that he'll probably end up with nothin', but at least he'll reap the seeds that he sows. It's a similar theme to the first album's 'Ramblin' Gamblin' Man', the Creedence Clearwater Revival sound (particularly John Fogerty's vocals), even the heavier bubblegum or organ-dominated garage sound of bands like Crazy Elephant and The Standells. Some critics rated it the best track on the album. As a single, it gave them a modest hit, reaching number 84, and became their second 45 release in the UK.

'Teachin' Blues' 2:00

Clocking in concisely at just two minutes, this takes the simplest of guitar and organ riffs, adds a few brief stop-start moments and works it for all it's worth, while Seger sings about how he's 'gonna roll and smoke and boogie and ball now'.

'Leanin' On My Dream' 3:17

Not for the first time on this album, with this song, Seger seems to be paying homage to Creedence, particularly in his vocal and in the lead guitar. This time, there's also a narrative about civil unrest on the streets, picket lines, people nearby shouting out 'Down with democracy' and a man grabbing his arm to ask him where he stands. When he gets home, he turns on the TV, with a riot taking place, and in the middle of it, he sees the same man being dragged away by the police, and one of them screams that he's leaning on his dream. Whether this relates to an event that Seger witnessed is anyone's guess, but it paints a vividly disturbing picture of protests in action.

'Mongrel Too' 4:08

The pace slows on this more restrained bluesy workout, in which the musical backbone comes from a simple piano riff and rarely deviates from one chord. The stream of consciousness lyrics say little, but towards the end, it builds dramatically with gospel-tinged backing vocals.

'River Deep – Mountain High' (Phil Spector, Jeff Barry, Ellie Greenwich) 7:26

The only song on this album not written by Seger is a live recording of the Ike and Tuna Turner favorite, a number three UK hit in 1966 that barely registered in the US top 100, although the sleeve has no information on date or venue. The System may have taken their cue either from Eric Burdon and The Animals, or from the initial lineup of Deep Purple, both of whom had recently released their own similarly extended versions. They likewise add their own instrumental breaks, on organ and then guitar, while Seger's hoarse vocal sounds like he is almost on the verge of imploding. The band remain pretty tight throughout the seven minutes, and as a performance, it's just as exciting as the best of the studio tracks on this album. Seger would do similar justice to Mr and Mrs Turner's other finest three minutes on 45 in the following decade, as history will show.

Non-Album Single

'Lookin' Back' 2:43 b/w **'Highway Child'** 2.49

Released in September 1971

Produced by Punch Andrews

Recorded during the *Mongrel* sessions but not used on the album, this followed just over a year later and was credited to Seger as a soloist, as The System were no more. A laid-back mid-paced number, with Skip Knape on particularly good form on Hammond organ, it features another defiant, angry lyric about 'too many people lookin' back', the reactionaries who accepted if not connived at the indefinite war in Vietnam, even when they still saw footage of soldiers dying and their reaction was to 'reach out and change the channel on the TV'. In a radio interview about four years later, he said it was 'written about all the people who wanted to retain the conservative ideas, as opposed to trying anything liberal or new. Plus, it had a double meaning about the band, too, and the music that had gone down.'

Another local success, it had limited release elsewhere, seemingly only in Canada, France and Sweden. Seger kept the song in his set for some years, and an in-concert version would appear on *'Live' Bullet*.

Bob Seger

Brand New Morning (1971)

Personnel:
Bob Seger: vocals, guitar, piano
Engineered by Milan Bogdan, mixed by Bogdan, Bob Seger and Punch Andrews
Release date: October 1971
Highest chart positions: US: did not chart
Running time: 31:32

One month after 'Lookin' Back', Seger released his first solo album. To general surprise, he now took a completely different direction – as a solo singer-songwriter. The title said it all. He had been perhaps losing confidence in his musical abilities as a frontman, as well as in his personal life. 'Big River' on *Mongrel* showed that he was longing to plough a more introspective furrow. The man who had become renowned as one of Detroit's hottest rock properties was ready to follow in the footsteps of Kris Kristofferson, Bob Dylan, Leonard Cohen and Joni Mitchell, all of whom he admired as 'people who write stuff that I can't even get close to.' It wasn't going to stop him from trying.

If it was a misstep or a total surprise, he had his reasons. Basically, he admitted, he simply wanted to step back and just write. David Teegarden, a drummer who worked on and off with him for several years, put it down to his being dissatisfied, or else getting stale with The System and wanting to try out an acoustic path.

This is a solo album in every sense of the word; just one man, his songs, his voice and either a six-string acoustic guitar or a piano every time, without any vocal or instrumental overdubs, let alone guest musicians. For the most part, his playing is purely functional, based mainly around the chords, so there's no revelation of another John Renbourn or Paul Simon on the strings, another Rick Wakeman or Keith Emerson on the keys. What he does has charm and simplicity, even if it's the last thing you'd expect from the man who gave us 'Ramblin' Gamblin' Man'. When Andrews heard the results, he was unenthusiastic, but knew better than to try to overrule him, so he just let him take control.

'Everyone has dour periods', Seger explained several years later to Robert Hilburn in the *Los Angeles Times,* and 'the acoustic album' was 'the depths' for him.

> I was alone. My marriage had broken up. There was no direction. I felt kind of defeated. But I didn't really have any option. I knew I wanted to play music. I just needed time to figure out how to go about it again.

Most of the songs are introspective, heartfelt and charming, if perhaps a little raw or naïve, and more likely to be sad than brimming over with excitement. They do show another side of his talent, one that would come to maturity a few years onwards. Rock 'n' roll it isn't, and it may verge on being a little too precious, too earnest, but it's impossible to dislike or dismiss. Yet it was clearly not the Seger album that fans or the label imagined they'd get from him.

One theory is that Capitol wanted to drop him because his record sales were performing below expectations, and needed a contract-filling album to help them complete the process. With the stresses in his personal and professional life, he didn't have it in him to fight any such decision. A fourth album that would sell only a fraction of what the previous ones had managed would make their decision and give him his freedom. He may have felt that he and The System could go no further, which adds credence to the theory that 'You Know Who You Are' was a subtle goodbye note. He would later claim that the album was really a collection of demos that he had submitted to the suits to prove that he had work in progress for the next one, and the next thing he knew was that they were releasing them without further embellishment.

Rumor has it that he came to hate it so much that he buried his copy, or the master tapes, depending on which version you believe, in his back garden. Maybe he felt a little embarrassed at having publicly revealed his inner self so much. If this was the case, he could at least take comfort in the fact that it sold so poorly. Like *Noah*, it was never released in Britain, and not outside the US and Canada, or at least until 'unofficial' CDs appeared in other countries in the 21st century. Nevertheless, the early 1970s was the era of the acoustic confessional singer-songwriter, with Cat Stevens and James Taylor at the peak of their success on both sides of the Atlantic. If some of Seger's local fanbase thought this was the shape of things to come, he certainly fitted the Stevens-Taylor template.

It was not unknown for rock singers to do a complete musical volte-face for various reasons. John Lennon's first solo album, *John Lennon/Plastic Ono Band*, released almost a year before, had been a painful exercise in soul-baring that bore no resemblance to what many fans were expecting from a former Beatle. Bruce Springsteen's *Nebraska*, which followed in 1982, trod a similar path. Yet the former featured additional musicians on most tracks, while the latter included a few instrumental overdubs from its creator. However, both of them were already well established in the musical profession by the time they made those records. As yet, Seger was still a relatively unknown quantity, and stardom was a long way ahead.

Talking of Lennon, in December 1971, Seger found himself sharing a concert billing with John and Yoko. The couple were headlining a Freedom Rally at the Crisler Arena, University of Michigan, for activist and manager of fellow Detroit rock band MC5, John Sinclair, who had been imprisoned for possession of two marijuana cigarettes. Others on the bill included Stevie Wonder, Phil Ochs and Commander Cody and The Lost Planet Airmen. It achieved its purpose, as Sinclair was released from prison shortly afterwards.

For a short time, it was apparent that Seger had not completely finished with his born-again singer-songwriter career. A couple of local radio presenters who had supported him from the start were involved with gigs that he played around this time. One, Peter Cavanaugh, had booked The Bob Seger System to close a show, and was rather surprised to learn that it would be the frontman – but not the band. Andrews advised him to put Seger early on the bill, as he was 'going to be real soft'. So Cavanaugh introduced him on stage, telling the audience that they were about to see his first-ever acoustic set. Seger came on with just his guitar, and they sat politely through the first two songs, but became restless after that. What had happened to their favorite rock 'n' roller? Another presenter, Dan Carlisle, also chatted to him backstage and discussed the last album with him. Seger said he was disappointed at how badly it had gone down. 'Well, you know it doesn't rock at all', was Carlisle's response.

'Brand New Morning' 3:23

This is the testament of a man who is sweeping the decks clean for the first day of the rest of his life. As one verse begins quite unequivocally with boldly-strummed chords on the guitar, 'Forget the past, you know that's ancient history, it's a time to be reborn'. Throughout, he sings almost defiantly, with the voice of a man determined to take on the world.

'Maybe Today' 3:11

'Maybe' is the keyword to the second lyric. In this ballad comes an expression of guarded optimism in the hope that he will find the one who touches his heart. However, the piano work is more ambitious than usual, with gentle melodic curves adding some light and shade between the chords, echoing Paul McCartney or Elton John.

'Sometimes' 5:11

Doubts and lack of faith intrude, as he sings in a voice that's part of the time, almost a whisper, then a cry of desperation. For the intro, and with brief interludes later on, he gives us some gentle guitar picking and then strums the chords more fiercely, as if in anger. It's probably a post-mortem on his brief, failed marriage, and what must be the saddest item on the record:

> Sometimes you laugh aloud, sometimes you're far away,
> Sometimes you just don't hear a single word a say
> Sometimes you just don't care at all

It's not to be confused with one of his later compositions of the same title that would follow 15 years later on *Like A Rock*.

'You Know Who You Are' 3:14

For the second track in a row, he demonstrates his anger as he seems to be pointing the finger at someone, probably his former bandmates in The System. In the opening lines, he sings as he strums the chords with feeling, 'It looked like it, it felt like it, but in the end it was just a show'. Were the three albums they made together and the gigs they did as bad as that? How else do we interpret the lines further on: 'The sound was bad I couldn't hear you, but then what were we doing on a stage?' Towards the end, his voice almost breaks with passion as he considers, 'It was such a close call I think that's why I'm writing this at all', and then returns to a whisper as he closes the song with the title.

'Railroad Days' 6:54
On the album's longest song, almost seven minutes, the singer taps his foot as he strums the guitar, reminiscing in a song that verges towards skiffle on his childhood, of 'railroad days, when the sun seemed to shine on its way'. The afternoons were spent playing ball and listening to The Drifters on the hi-fi during summer nights – life was free. Oh, for the good old days. Of course, nothing lasts forever, and it ends with him coming back to cruel reality, hearing as an adult that only yesterday they shut the trains down, the ones that ran past the field where he used to play.

'Louise' 2:50
Even closer to foot-tapping skiffle, this may not be the most significant or the deepest song on the album, and might at first come across as a bit of a throwaway, but it sounds like he and his guitar are having fun as he delivers a Woody Guthrie-like romp. Louise, the daughter of a preacher and a former nun, is a rebel against convention for its own sake, a free spirit who thinks more of riding on a Harley with her boyfriend than doing her homework.

'Song For Him' 4:33
A slower, moodier piece, this hints at gospel and the presence of a higher power. The guitar opens the song softly for the first verse, gathering force as he hits the strings with more purpose on the second verse. There's no explicit reference in the lyrics to a deity, but lines like 'He's with me at the break of dawn, he's every star that shines at night' offer the suggestion. Perhaps more than any of the other seven tracks, this would have been enhanced by a nod to some spiritual backing vocals.

'Something Like' 3:26
To conclude comes another slower guitar-backed song with hope for a better future. 'If she means so much to you, there's not a thing you shouldn't do', he sings, 'If it will help to show her that you care'. Yet, with these expressions of love, or at least 'something like loving', comes a kind of sequel to the first number, with its anticipation of 'A brand new morning, a brand new day, a brand new chance to make it all work out some way'. Twenty-five seconds before the end comes a neat touch of picking before he hits the final chords.

Smokin' O.P.'s (1972)

Personnel:
Bob Seger: vocals, guitar, piano
Skip Knape: organ, keyboards, bass pedals, piano
David Teegarden: drums, maracas, marimba
Jack Ashford: percussion, tambourine
Eddie 'Bongo' Brown: percussion, conga
Mike Bruce: guitar
Jim Bruzzese: tambourine
Dan Honaker: bass
Carl Lagassa: guitar
Pep Perrine: drums
Chrystal Jenkins, Pam Todd: backing vocals
Al Yungton: string arrangement
Produced by Punch Andrews
Recorded at Pampa Studios, Warren, Michigan; RCA Studios, Toronto
Record label: Reprise (UK), Palladium (US)
Release date: August 1972
Highest chart position: UK: did not chart, US: 180
Running time: 33:59

Seger's return to the sound for which he was best known, even if his fame had still barely spread outside his home ground, would not be long in coming. Capitol had let their contract with him expire without discussing a renewal, and Andrews negotiated a three-album deal with Warner Bros/Reprise Records. In the US, these were released on Andrews' own short-lived Palladium label.

For his next album, he recorded what was basically a trio of himself, keyboard player Skip Knape and drummer David Teagarden, plus further musicians (including Honaker, Lagassa and Perrine from the earlier bands) and backing singers, for a collection of songs consisting mostly of cover versions. His idea was to pay homage to some of his favorites on the contemporary scene and a couple of his heroes, and record an album that would be fun to make as well as good to listen to. The title was a play on words, which could be interpreted as 'Smokin' other people's cigarettes', or else a set of really 'Smokin'' tunes by other people, or O.P.'s. This inspired a sleeve design by Tom Weschler, the group's roadie and official photographer, based on the red and green design of a packet of Lucky Strike cigarettes, incorporating Seger's name and the album title. There would only be one original new song, or two original Seger numbers if the return of his best-loved nearly-hit is included.

Noting that this was, as a solo performer, the first British release for the man whom Detroit journalist Dave Marsh of *Creem* rated as highly as John Fogerty, *Let It Rock* praised 'Heavy Music' as a classic while calling the rest 'straightforward, relaxed, mid-1960s white soul, funky-butt music, nice but not the stuff that myths are made of.'

'Bo Diddley' (Elias McDaniel) 6:17
The album's opening cut, and also the longest, is in effect a jam session with Seger and the band on that unmistakable chink-a-chink-chink syncopated rhythm. They start off on the original song named 'Bo Diddley'. After that, guitar and organ take their turns for soloing while the rhythm section lays down the beat, with both former instruments both cutting out for a little while at one stage. A little less than five minutes in, they segue into Diddley's next best-remembered number, 'Who Do You Love', and then for a few seconds everything stops but the organ, to play four descending chords – the only time the whole track deviates from a single chord, in fact. They finish up on another verse and chorus, and then come to a tidy end. Six minutes is just about the right length for them to keep the jamming in progress before there's any risk of losing the listener's attention. The 'Who Do You Love' section, lasting two minutes and 13 seconds, was issued as the album's second single without charting.

'Love The One You're With' (Stephen Stills) 4:17
The Stills classic had been a US top 20 hit the previous year for its writer (and his only top 40 success in the UK), and a little later for The Isley Brothers. Like the first track on the album, it also broadly follows the Bo Diddley beat, and it might have been more effective coming later on the album. Having said that, this is probably every bit as good as the original, with Crystal Jenkins and Pam Todd contributing as much to the vocals as the main man himself.

'If I Were A Carpenter' (Tim Hardin) 3:47
This was the second song in a row to have been familiar as a recent hit for other acts. Yet Seger still brings a fresh, soulful angle to the lyrics, while it features what is probably Skip Knape's finest organ work on the album. The three other best-known versions – from Bobby Darin, The Four Tops and Johnny Cash & June Carter – had already made the US top 40 during the previous six years, with the two former taking it into the UK top ten as well. Seger's version also came out as a single and reached number 76 in the US.

'Hummin' Bird' (Leon Russell) 3:46
Seger opens the song singing the first verse unaccompanied for the first 25 seconds or so before the band come in behind him. Piano and organ carry it through for the most part, although the guitar takes a solo after the first chorus. It's a relaxed love song, again bringing the more soulful side of Seger to the fore, with a hint of the blues. Also, maybe it's the common Leon Russell factor, but the gospel feel on this song provided by the Jenkins-Todd duo's backing vocals makes one realize that, as a singer, Seger's soulful, rasping voice bore some similarities to that of Joe Cocker.

'Let It Rock' (Edward Anderson) 3:25

No self-respecting rocker from that era can resist covering something by the master, Chuck Berry having used his middle names as a songwriting alias for this one. Originally recorded by him in 1959 and a minor hit the following year in the US, it was subsequently recorded by many others on both sides of the Atlantic, notably The Rolling Stones, Jerry Garcia, Dave Edmunds and George Thorogood & The Destroyers. Seger and his band roar through this one at full throttle, and it sounds like he's double-tracking his vocal on the second verse. In addition to the inevitable guitar breaks, Skip adds an impressive passage on organ about halfway through. The song would also be reprised on both of Seger's live albums within the next few years.

'Turn On Your Love Light' (Deadric Malone, Joseph Wade Scott) 4:44

First recorded by Bobby Bland in 1961, the song became a favorite for many other major names, including The Grateful Dead, Them and Jerry Lee Lewis. On another energetic soul belter, Seger's vocal shares the honors with Skip's lively organ work.

'Jesse James' (traditional, arr. Seger) 3:26

In the first few seconds, you could be forgiven for thinking this is a Beatles rehearsal for 'Get Back', with those touches on organ and, above all, the military-style rolling snare drum beat as used by Ringo Starr on the song. 'Jesse James', telling the tale of a 19th-century outlaw who robbed the rich to help the poor, has been a much-loved song since its first recording in 1919. In contrast to the folk and country treatments, this rocks at a furious pace, hammered along by Teegarden.

'Someday' 2:31

After a helping of other people's songs, the album finishes off with two Seger originals, although one was already well-known to fans. Seger can be a master of springing total surprises, and rarely more so than on what is his only new original song on the collection. It's back to the introspective songwriter, not the all-out rock 'n' roller. On first listen, it sounds as though it could be an outtake from *Brand New Morning*, apart from the presence of strings. He sits at his piano, musing softly in ballad style, about never having quite kept up with the rest, but somehow he'll bear that heavy load, and keep on reaching for the sun. It's a pleasantly relaxing interlude, if nothing more.

'Heavy Music' 2:28

So we return full circle to where Seger arrived, in his early days with The Last Heard. There's no clue on the label or sleeve as to whether this is a re-recording of the 1967 performance on Cameo-Parkway or not, but that seems unlikely. It's safe to assume that nobody still had access to the original tape, and as it was in mono, it was re-channeled in stereo from an old 45 for this album, or so the story goes. Nobody apparently went to court claiming copyright infringement. Listen carefully on a high-quality sound system and some surface noise will be apparent.

Back In '72 (1973)

Personnel:
Bob Seger: guitar, vocals
Jack Ashford: maracas, marimba, tambourine
Barry Beckett: organ, piano, electric piano, RMI electronic piano, Mellotron
Philip Bliss: steel guitar
Eddie 'Bongo' Brown: percussion, conga
J. J. Cale: lead guitar
Pete Carr, Jimmy Johnson, Bill Mueller: guitar
Tom Cartmell: flute, saxophone
Roger Hawkins, Jamie Oldaker: drums
David Hood: bass
Sergio Pastora: conga, tambourine, timbales
Dick Sims: organ, piano, clavinet, pedal bass
Scherrie Brown, Marcy Levy: backing vocals
Recorded at Paradise Studios, Tijuana, Oklahoma; Pampa Studios, Warren, Michigan; Muscle Shoals Sound Studios, Sheffield, Alabama
Record label: Reprise (UK), Palladium (US)
Release date: January 1973
Highest chart position: UK: did not chart, US: 188
Running time: 35:10

Just before the Smokin' O.P.'s team went their separate ways, Teegarden and Knape introduced Seger to the two musicians who would replace them. Drummer Jamie Oldaker and keyboard player Dick Sims would form the core of his group for the next album to be recorded. They were briefly known as The Borneo Band, although not credited thus on the record.

After the covers on *Back In '72*, Seger gave priority to original material, with six of the nine songs being his own. Prior to making the album, he had been playing dates around the country with Oldaker, Sims and Hood, and they had really gelled. Nevertheless, while the quartet had a good working relationship together, Teegarden thought that their frontman was too timid when they were on stage and didn't really project himself properly. Detroit disc jockey Dan Carlisle thought he seemed a little 'afraid of the audience', although he wouldn't admit it, and didn't slip naturally into the role of Mr Rock Star.

> He didn't really like being the spotlight person; he was the reluctant star. He was a good songwriter, and he loved the music, and he was good at it. What I think held him back a lot was that, unlike Ted Nugent, he wasn't a live wire, personality-wise.

Others had told him that he was a good performer live, but came across as too shy. He took this advice on board. Around this time, he began watching the young, new Bruce Springsteen, talking about him and evidently learning from his example. When he recruited another guitarist, it gave him the freedom to put his instrument down and concentrate on singing. Having to play and do vocals at the same time had made him 'a real prisoner.' Now he could put on more of a show. 'A weight was lifted from my shoulder when I stopped playing lead guitarist', he said. 'I started developing as a singer and concentrated on the performance aspect of my career.'

He gradually gained in confidence and found himself slipping with relish into being a really effective frontman on stage, almost rivalling the likes of Mick Jagger and Roger Daltrey. Now he could take the spotlight and whip the crowd up into a frenzy, running around the stage and pointing at the audience to try to get them going. He could also spontaneously turn around to point at the guitarist or any of the other musicians behind him when he thought it was time for them to take a solo.

Above all, he could focus much more on the craft of songwriting. Before that, he was writing nearly all his songs in the style of 'great riffs', like Jimi Hendrix, Eric Clapton and Jimmy Page. 'To me, that was somewhat of a cop-out because I was building songs around a riff, and that's all there was.' At last, he could give adequate attention to writing songs with melody and more interesting structures.'

One of the backing vocalists, Marci (Marcy) Levy (aka Marcella Detroit), would later join Eric Clapton's band and then Shakespears Sister. Among the other musicians appearing on record with him were the long-established session band, The Muscle Shoals Rhythm Section, for only three tracks. Their original deal with him was to play for a fee of $1500 a side. He understood this to mean the price per album side, and only after they had started working together did he realize that they meant the figure quoted was the fee per song. After that, he had to let them go for the rest of the sessions, although he would call upon them again in the future.

Rolling Stone journalist Jon Landau loved the album, writing that Seger belonged at the very top of the rock 'n' roll heap, and this would be 'just the record to put him there.' In later years, Seger was very disparaging about it. He conceded that there were a couple of decent songs there, but he was never satisfied with the sound of his voice, and he thought the mix was awful. After his contract with Warner/Reprise expired, he bought back the rights to all three albums he had made with them. The other two were briefly reissued, but not this one. It's now as rare as the first four Capitol long players, long since deleted and never having been officially made available again. Some call it 'one of the great lost albums' of the era. Others feel that Seger's musical reputation might have stood a little higher if only all seven of his pre-1975 albums had remained available throughout his career and never been deleted.

'Midnight Rider' (Gregg Allman, Robert Payne) 2:45

The Allman Brothers' original version in 1971 never charted, and it was left to Joe Cocker to issue the first version that did in the US, a top 30 hit late the following year. It would have done so around the same time that Seger was in the studios recording the same song. Both men succeed in transforming it into a gruff, wild soul belter, given added power by the backing vocalists. Here, Seger gives it more of a blue-eyed soul rhythm, strongly reminiscent of the feel that Joe brought to his groundbreaking version of 'The Letter' two years earlier, and he also has the benefit of some wonderfully relaxed, almost jazzy, guitar work from J. J. Cale. Joe's funky workout on the Allman Brothers' song is quite ahead of its time in anticipating much of the disco sound that would fill the charts two or three years hence.

'So I Wrote You A Song' 2:44
The writer of heartfelt ballads was now coming into his own. Here, Seger sits at the piano, pouring his heart out to a loved one about whom he has been dreaming all day, so a song particularly for her is in order. Organ, unobtrusive drums, charming backing vocals and especially Bliss's tender steel guitar all add to the romantic mood.

'The Stealer' (Andy Fraser, Paul Rodgers, Paul Kossoff) 2:55
Seger was an early convert to the music of Paul Rodgers and Free, and loved this track, the surprisingly unsuccessful follow-up single to 'All Right Now'. He was not the only one – Rod Stewart and The Faces also featured it regularly on stage. Paul Kossoff's original guitar solo was always going to be a hard act to follow, but the band all pull it off in style. Seger brings the required grit to the vocals, and Rodgers was suitably impressed with this treatment of the song.

'Rosalie' 3:22
After one major band on the other side of the Atlantic, Free, found that Seger had covered one of their tunes, another band in the same part of the world gained some mileage and later a top 20 hit with one of his songs. He knew that writing a song in tribute to one of North America's most powerful figures in radio would be as good a way as any of getting one of his songs broadcast. Rosalie Trombley was a well-respected music director at CKLW, an AM radio station based in Windsor, Ontario, and several acts of the time owed their initial breaks to her support, the woman who was, according to the lyrics, 'everybody's favorite little record girl', a woman who's 'got the power, a smoother operator you will never see'. This is the best example of Seger's storming rock 'n' roll style on the album, and listeners might detect similarity between this and a later Elton John hit, 'The Bitch Is Back'. Ireland's premier hard rock export Thin Lizzy recorded an equally powerful version on their 1975 album *Fighting*, although it failed to chart. It took an even more spirited, rather faster performance on their 1978 in concert album *Live And Dangerous*, integrated with a brief snatch of their own 'Cowgirl's Song', to make the song a number 20 hit in the UK.

'Turn The Page' 5:11

Often regarded as one of Seger's finest lyrics ever, and not only by himself, this is a slow, introspective song about the ups and downs of a life on the road. Although he wrote it from a musician's point of view, he said it was basically inspired by his feelings of weariness on the road, and it could equally be for travelling businessmen, truck drivers, or anyone who had to travel long distances, and miss their home and family. One of the catalysts for creating it was after the band had been harassed after stopping to refuel at about two in the morning by another batch of people there. The band were sometimes treated with derision because of their hippie-like looks, so this time they had stuffed their long hair up in their hats. Even so, it was noticed, and they had to put up with snide comments and laughter as the other customers sneeringly cast doubts on their gender. After another gig the following night, Seger told the others that he had just gotten another line for a song that he had been working on for a while. It was about walking into a restaurant, with the feeling that he was being watched, and he really wanted to explode:

> Most times you can't hear 'em talk, other times you can
> All the same old clichés, is it woman is it man?

Other lines in the song referred to a feeling of wishing the journey was over, or lying in bed with the echoes of the amplifiers still ringing in his head.

The instruments used include Mellotron and saxophone, the latter played by Chris Cartmell, who would become one of Seger's most regular musicians. When they were preparing the song, Tom Weschler told him to try to imagine that he was on the Bowery in New York City, at 3 am, under a street lamp. 'There's a light mist coming down. You're all by yourself. Show me what that sounds like'. The musician thought for a moment, then played the haunting notes of what would become the intro.

Seger and his band recorded the song four times in three years 'until we finally got the cut.' Andrews hated it, saying, 'it's too down, it's too dark', but it was Seger's favorite song on the album. Many years later, he told Ken Sharp of *Classic Rock* that he never thought it would last as long as it had, and it really 'captured something'. Though never a single, it was also loved by fans, becoming one of the numbers that they always had to play live or else audiences would get very disappointed. Some rock critics have called it one of the definitive lyrics about life on the road. Australian singer Joe English had a hit with his version down under in 1974, and it has also subsequently been recorded by Waylon Jennings, Golden Earring and Metallica.

'Back In '72' 4:25

The title track is a rousing number about looking back on good times in the past, but as the album was recorded in 1972, maybe not that long previously.

There is a brief reference to 'Tricky Dick', President Nixon, still at the height of his powers, just before the Watergate scandal broke. Also a line near the end – 'When the waters cleared it was what we feared, we learned nothing new' – was one that reflected his thoughts that 1972 had been 'a kinda nothin' year where nothing major happened.' Musically, it's a good-time groove that deviates very little from three chords, and, in fact, uses the same chord throughout on the verses, but when the music is as infectious as the guitar and sax driving this one along, simple is good.

'Neon Sky' 3:35

It now becomes evident what an album of contrasts this is. One moment it's swaggering rock or funk, then it falls back to remarkable restraint. The sight of a neon sky seems to hold memories for the singer, memories of an affair long ago. Underpinning the story is a gloriously subtle arrangement with a two-note phrase on bass, restrained drumming, velvety electric piano and sparse, eerie notes from slide guitar in the verses, with a tougher guitar and drum sound joining in on the chorus and then cutting back out.

'I've Been Working' (Van Morrison) 4:33

The original first appeared on Morrison's 1970 album *His Band And The Street Choir*. His recording verges towards jazz-funk territory, and Seger's raspy vocals, plus a superbly flowing guitar solo and the interplay of piano, organ and funky guitar riffs, retain the flavor. He said that he loved Morrison's 'dream-like, trance-like' singing style and jazz-like method of 'winging it'. The latter was not Seger's greatest fan, and once claimed in an interview that he and Springsteen were both ripping him off.

'I've Got Time' 5:40

After several upbeat numbers, the album's longest track provides a peaceful conclusion, a song of self-discovery. The introspective lyrics are largely autobiographical, from a boy born in the final days of the Second World War. He was lucky in that his father had not been called up to fight, but still had a difficult childhood, 'raised and taught to hurry', went through a period of self-doubt, and only now, as he grows older, does he learn 'how to run the race'. Once he had no reason for living, everything he did was wrong, but at last he has found someone who made his whole life shine. The restrained backing complements the mood perfectly, with soft lead guitar and flute-like sounds prominent, and the drums working up a little steam in the instrumental break while holding back well for the rest of the song.

Seven (1974)

Personnel:
The Silver Bullet Band
Bob Seger: guitar, vocals
Drew Abbott: lead guitar
Tom Cartmell: saxophone
Rick Manasa: organ, piano
Robin Robbins: Mellotron
Chris Campbell: bass
Charlie Allen Martin: drums
Additional musicians:
Dave Doran, Bill Mueller: lead guitar
Jim McCarthy: lead guitar, slide guitar
Charlie McCoy: rhythm guitar
David Briggs, Bobby Woods: piano
John Harris: organ
Tommy Cogbill: bass
Kenny Buttrey, Randy Myers: drums
Produced by Punch Andrews, Bob Seger
Recorded at Quadrophonic Sound, Nashville
Record label: Reprise (UK), Palladium (US)
Recorded: 1973
Release date: March 1974
Highest chart position: UK: NR, US: did not chart
Running time: 31:00

Following an album that had its share of reflective singer-songwriter fare, Seger returned to mainly full-tilt rock 'n' roll on his seventh (hence the title). He was gradually gathering the right mix of musicians around him for studio and stage, and now that he had an additional guitarist, he could devote more attention to coming up with new material for new albums and their live repertoire. 'I sort of stopped being a songwriter, stopped being creative and just tried to be a lead guitar player more than anything else', he commented about his previous situation. It was time for a change.

Following Weschler's design for *Smokin' O.P.'s*, the artwork for *Seven* was also initially to be inspired by a product of consumer packaging – a painting of a Seagram's 7 bottle of whisky, retitled Seger's 7. This time, plans fell through. They contacted the Seagram company, who raised no objection as long as their name was not included in the design. Band and management were sure that Seagram would be pleased with what could perhaps be regarded as free promotion for them, and maybe hoped for a few free samples. When the artwork was completed and sent to Warner Bros, a couple of days before the cover was to go to press, it was immediately rejected as bosses were sure that Seagram would take them to court. When assured that permission for the idea had been granted, Warners insisted that if they wanted the album to be released, they had to think of something else. Weschler was accordingly sent to come up with the abstract design in bold colors, which was accepted.

Initial copies of *Seven* included the word 'Contrasts' below the artwork on the front of the sleeve. This led some to assume that the title of the album was *Seven Contrasts*, and subsequent pressings dropped the word from the design. Later, when it became unavailable, a bootleg version appeared with the title *Seven Worlds*.

The last of the three albums under the Warner/Reprise deal, *Seven* also saw the beginnings of what would become The Silver Bullet Band, comprising guitarist Drew Abbott, sax man Chris Cartmell, organist Robyn (formerly Robin) Robbins, bassist Chris Campbell and drummer Charlie Martin. The next few releases would be credited jointly to singer and band, and on tour, they would be billed thus. As Martin said around this time, they were, for a while, the regular Bob Seger Band throughout 1974 and onwards. Then somebody commented that Seger was like the Lone Ranger, who had the silver bullets. From that, it was a short step to giving his band their name.

'Get Out Of Denver' 2:42

Everyone involved hits the ground running with one of the greatest Chuck Berry songs that Chuck never wrote. In this, Seger penned a carefree anthem for youth on the road, although there is a darker undertone. Friends are driving at full speed through Nebraska, heading for the mountains, stopping briefly for a 'line on somethin' heavy' from 'a Baptist preachin' southern funky school teacher'. Then enter the cops, who tell them to leave because 'you look just like a commie and you might just be a member'. The era of Senator Joseph McCarthy's witch hunts against 'the reds' was still a recent memory for those who had lived through the 1950s.

As a single, it gave Seger another modest entry on the top 100 at number 80. Andrews insisted that they would release it as a single, much to Bob's annoyance. One day, he entered the office while Andrews was out and found Weschler there instead. Bob asked him what he thought, and when Weschler said he thought it a good idea, Bob told him he could have any royalties, picked up a piece of paper, wrote a brief note to that effect, signed it and gave it to him. Whether Andrews took advantage of the gesture or threw the note in the bin isn't recorded.

The song would soon come to be recognized as a pub rock classic staple. In Britain, Eddie and The Hot Rods covered it on their EP *Live At The Marquee* in 1976, playing it even faster than the original. In doing so, they gave Seger his first UK top 50 hit as a writer, as well as becoming the first new wave band to appear on BBC TV's *Top Of The Pops* when they opened the show with it on 9 September that year. Other British versions would come from Dave Edmunds and Status Quo, who had played on the same bill as Bob and The Silver Bullet

Band in America not long before and said they were one of the best acts they had ever worked with. Years later, Rick Parfitt commented in a webchat that 'they were like us on stage, the entire band was into it and working, which I'd always seen as Quo's forte.' In 1994, the night that Seger was inducted into the Rock and Roll Hall of Fame, Bob Dylan was playing a gig at the State Theatre in Detroit, where he performed the song and dedicated it to the writer.

'Long Song Comin' 4:26
Seger's not done with baiting the establishment yet. A politician is about to make a speech, shuffling his notes, while the audience – well, at least the singer and his companion – wish they had left as they're trapped in the room and have better things to do. The next butt of his disdain is an eager lady from the church bazaar, all smiles, who gets up to speak her piece on behalf of her mission. Again, it looks like a long song is coming, and nobody really wants to listen. This little ode to impatience and being in the wrong place is set to a snarling, Rolling Stones-like delivery with some biting lead guitar and saxophone – with a bit of a nod to 'Honky Tonk Women'.

'Need Ya' 3:20
The Stones' influence feeds into this third song as well, although there's nothing complicated to the lyrics, only love, or is it lust that's driving 'a loving man of the world' insane? A bustling rhythm with jaunty piano and slide guitar makes the perfect complement to Seger's breathless vocal delivery.

'School Teacher' 2:43
Much the same goes for the next number. The band complement Seger again well enough on a tight, simple number, on which the guitar, piano and drums chug along at a brisk pace while he works himself up into a frenzy on the object of his desire.

'Cross Of Gold' 2:20
Musically, shades of the throbbing Bo Diddley beat resurface on this song. The cauldron of organ and guitar bubbles at a frantic pace as Bob takes a swipe in his lyrics at greed, power and, by association with the title, maybe even Christianity itself, though there are no overt references to religion. 'You can change the way you live', reads the opening line. By the third verse, he is singing about keeping the people down, taking the best there is, and building shelters underground.' Basically, it comes across as a sharp critique of human greed, power and manipulation. A lively tune, it carries quite an uncompromising message.

'U.M.C. [Upper Middle Class]' 3:12
Seger hasn't finished with social comment yet, but this time he does it with a grin on his face. A relaxed shuffle with piano and bass keeping the bottom

line going, the drums and organ adding a few flashes of fire, cruises along to a list of all the good things he wants in life that will make him a member of that esteemed rank. These include a cottage on the river, evenings spent drinking the best Burgundy, fancy suits, a yacht and a pretty secretary taking dictation while sitting on his knee – and he'll pretend to be a liberal but still support the Republican party. It's a joke, but quite a pleasant one.

It was released as a non-charting single in November 1974, with 'This Old House' on the B-side. The latter song never appeared on an album, but was partly 'rewritten' a couple of years later with some of the chord sequence and completely different lyrics as 'We've Got Tonite (Tonight)'.

'Seen A Lot Of Floors' 2:57

Probably the nearest thing to filler on here, this is a relaxed piano and drums-driven number in which he sings of trying to get rid of unwanted company. The guitar and sax solos add some necessary bite, but it's one of his less inspired moments.

'20 Years From Now' 4:30

Most of the tracks on this album would fit under the general label of rock 'n' roll, but not this one. Certainly the most heartfelt tune, it's another example of how well piano and organ complement each other on Seger's slower numbers. Two lovers are growing old together, whether going for a swim in the blue lagoon, listening all night to the wind, or just enjoying the song of the crickets. This shows yet again the path that would lead to some of his most treasured romantic tunes in the years ahead.

'All Your Love' 4:27

This inches a little closer to pure pop territory, and the lyrics don't go so deep, but it's an enjoyable end to the album. A gentle rocker driven by rhythm guitar that calls 'Get Back' to mind, playful touches on piano and a couple of stinging guitar solos, it pulls off a neat trick when the last verse and chorus finish a little over halfway through. Cue a false ending and then an extended guitar and piano break, which almost fade away and then return in full force for the finale. The Pointer Sisters kept close to the original's arrangement when they included it on their rock covers album *Priority* four years later.

Beautiful Loser (1975)

Personnel:
Bob Seger: lead vocals, guitar, slide guitar, harmonica, piano
The Silver Bullet Band:
Drew Abbott: guitar
Chris Campbell: bass
Charlie Martin: drums
Robin Robbins: organ
Muscle Shoals Rhythm Section:
Barry Beckett: grand piano, organ, synthesizer, electric piano
Pete Carr: lead and acoustic guitar
Roger Hawkins: drums, percussion
David Hood: bass
Jimmy Johnson: rhythm guitar
Spooner Oldham: organ, electric piano
Muscle Shoals Horn Section:
Harrison Calloway: trumpet
Ron Eades: baritone saxophone
Charles Rose: trombone
Harvey Thompson: tenor saxophone
Additional musicians:
Kenny Bell: guitar
Tom Cartmell: saxophone
Paul Kingery: guitar solo
Robyn Robbins: Mellotron
Stoney & Rocky: backing vocals
Produced by Bob Seger, Punch Andrews and Muscle Shoals Rhythm Section
Recorded at Muscle Shoals, Sheffield, Alabama
Release date: April 1975
Highest chart positions: UK: did not chart, US: 131
Certification: 2x Platinum
Running time: 33:01

Because of his admiration for Little Feat, who were on Warner Bros., Seger had relished becoming part of the same organization. Despite that, it never worked out for him as well as he hoped. 'Talk about getting lost in the woods', he said later. 'They had so many acts on the label that you just got lost in the shuffle. I felt like a number.' (That last sentence would recur almost word for word in a future song title.) The parting of the ways was evidently a mutual decision, especially when Warners rejected his next album, *Beautiful Loser*.

A new deal was necessary, and after a showcase for record executives at a hotel in Beverly Hills, Seger returned to Capitol. It proved a wise move, for he would stay with the company up to his last release over 40 years later. The success for which he had striven for so long, eager to break out beyond being number one in Detroit but almost totally unknown anywhere else, was just around the corner. When the record industry hit bad times during the decades to come, and once-fashionable acts were liable to find their contracts terminated after disappointing sales of their latest release, he would have nothing to fear.

The record was his eighth album and by general consent his strongest yet. Warner's loss was thus Capitol's gain. A major promotional effort by the label secured opening tour slots with Bachman Turner Overdrive and KISS at the top of the bill, and over the next few months, sold-out homecoming shows at Cobo and Olympia arenas, at which Bob and his band would be the star attraction.

In a radio interview at this time, he said that the new record was 'a concept album, to a degree', and that seven of the songs – everything but 'Jody Girl' and 'Nutbush City Limits' – all had a connected theme. Basically, they were in some way either about life on the road and his concept of what a winner or a loser is in life, as opposed to just the music business. 'Some of the songs talk about how we maintain our sanity – some of the songs are darker, about the loneliness.'

The overall mood of the album is mellow, introspective and sentimental in parts, but with two masterful rockers carefully spaced out between the other songs with their varying degrees of gentleness and subtlety. Anyone coming to this album after being familiar with some of the harder-rocking tracks from the next stage of his career might find it a little laid-back, if not disappointing at first, and then appreciate it far more after a few plays. The majority of it doesn't 'rock', but when it does, it does so with tremendous subtlety, not to say finesse.

Beautiful Loser was only a modest success at first outside Michigan, but after five of the nine tracks entered the band's setlist on live gigs and appeared on the subsequent live album, sales took off nationally and remained steady for some time. On re-signing their prodigal son, Capitol were rewarded with a real slow burner – and it would turn out to be only the beginning. When it was released, Seger was approaching the end of his 30th year. He was anything but an overnight sensation, but over almost a decade of records that barely raised their heads above the parapet, it was all about to happen. In his case, perhaps life did really begin at 30.

'Beautiful Loser' 3:26

Backing band: Muscle Shoals Rhythm Section

The title track, or rather the title itself and not the song, was inspired by the name of Leonard Cohen's novel, *Beautiful Losers,* and Seger's belief that it would be perfect as the starting point for a lyric. He was also very struck by one of Leonard's lines, 'He's reaching for the sky just to surrender', from 'The Stranger Song'. For him, it became a vehicle to write something about underachievers, people who set their goals so low that they never achieve anything. When people thought that he had written it about himself, he was at pains to stress that it wasn't. While he drew on his own experiences as so many other songwriters did, he said that he very rarely wrote about himself, and didn't regard himself as 'auteuristic'. 'I'm not like my songs at all. I'm a lot more upbeat than what I write.'

In an interview with *Music Connection* almost 20 years later, he said that he had never written a complete set of lyrics and then tried to build the music around them. 'A feel or a verse or a chorus' was the starting point, and lyrics would follow after he'd decided that a certain pattern, groove, or rhythm would be suitable. Then he would begin singing anything that came into his head, until he found a lyrical idea that would fit the ideas he had started out with. A different approach would be to tell himself, 'I wanna write a song about this.' That was the case here. Having chosen the title, it took him three or four unsatisfactory writes over the course of a year before coming up with the one that really worked.

It's a mid-tempo tune, part country and almost soulful ballad. Maybe it was significant that he had given the young Glenn Frey so much encouragement in the early days, and now his long-standing friend was one of the frontmen of the Eagles, on the verge of becoming the most successful band of mid-1970s America; he was helping to inspire the man who was a good three years his senior. Seger was now equally close to the other main Eagle, Don Henley, and something of their musical style was running off on him. He admitted he was writing songs more in an Eagles vein, and Frey was giving him greater confidence, telling him that he had been writing for about 12 years but was improving by leaps and bounds. Seger knew in his heart of hearts that he wasn't writing 'riff rockers' anymore. The former lead guitarist was now writing narrative songs. He played 'Beautiful Loser' while it was in progress to an admiring Frey, who helped him to tweak it in the final stages. There were four versions of the song, he said; one a ballad, one a blues, but he couldn't get quite the right tone on any of them. Frey was the first person to hear it while it was in the making, and 'stuck with the song until it all got pieced together.' It was also Frey who encouraged his old friend to expand his writing in further directions, and 'do something diverse.'

'Black Night' 3:19

Backing band: Muscle Shoals Rhythm Section

No relation to the old Deep Purple favorite, but a swaggering, growling song that puts us back in Rolling Stones territory. There's an interesting story in the ominous lyrics, perhaps a warning to a loved one that a spurned lover from her past is about to reappear. Rhythm guitar and electric piano are prominent in the backing, and there's a neat touch with a false ending after about two minutes before taking flight for another 60 seconds with a really mean guitar solo.

'Katmandu' 6:08

Backing band: Muscle Shoals Rhythm Section and Muscle Shoals Horn Section

The album's longest track is undoubtedly the most fun, and if you like the singer in full force rock 'n' roll mode, it's the star of the show. Katmandu was the capital of Nepal. In the 1960s, it had a reputation as the ultimate getaway destination, a remote and exotic location. For its writer, the name evoked a light-hearted desire to disappear there, for a complete rest from the hard work of constant touring and record company politics, somewhere so far away that nobody could bother him. He admitted it was meant to be somewhat tongue-in-cheek: 'You know, if you'd gone through what I've gone through, you'd want to go to Katmandu, too.' One has to smile at the reference to his former record company (who had rejected the album) in the second verse: 'Warner Brothers are such good hosts, I raise my whisky glass and give 'em a toast'. He likened it to 'Turn The Page' in calling it 'an exasperated song'. It was his way of saying in self-deprecation that he was never going to make it, so he might as well vanish to the most remote place possible. He had written it at the end of a period when he felt he was going nowhere fast. '*Beautiful Loser* was a transitional album, and in the song 'Katmandu', I still had some of that defeatist mentality, and you can hear it in there.'

Abbott unleashes his inner Chuck Berry on the guitar, Seger plays slide guitar and harmonica during one of the breaks (and maybe piano throughout as well, though the credits don't specify him) and the four musicians from the Muscle Shoals Horn Section pile on the delights. Much of the song makes do with three chords until four minutes in, when a couple more add a subtle twist to the tune. For the last minute or so until fading, all the musicians seem to be jamming together and are doubtless having the time of their lives. A three-minute edit gave Seger his first top 50 single (number 43) since 'Ramblin' Gamblin Man', although one can be forgiven for not wanting to hear the shorter version ever again after being familiar with the full glory of the complete opus.

The song would later be much in demand for use on soundtracks, among them *Mask* (1985), *Last Fling* (1987) and TV dramas including *Freaks And Geeks*, *Supernatural* and a documentary, *Journey To Everest* (2009).

'Jody Girl' 3:38

Here comes the first of the heartfelt ballads, a subdued folksy number with Van Morrison-like overtones. It's powered largely, but with restraint, by Seger's soothing acoustic guitar and piano, with Robbins on Mellotron, the only other musician featured. Lyrically, it's a song that could have been inspired by a former sweetheart, or equally pure fiction. Jody is now married and sitting at home 'watching clocks spin the hours away' with a soap opera on TV, while the old man is working and the children are out playing. It's a sad, humdrum existence when compared to carefree days at high school, with boyfriends knocking on her door. The feeling is that she's a woman who had great potential and a tremendous future, and has sacrificed everything for an unfulfilling family life. Moreover, whatever happened to that crazy boy with the lovelight in his eyes? Could he be the song's narrator, sadly looking at her from afar?

'Travelin' Man' 2:41
Backing band: Muscle Shoals Rhythm Section
In the previous decade, Seger introduced himself on the first Seger System album as a 'ramblin' gamblin' man'. According to this song, he hasn't changed. He's leaving his home and his friends, all the women are trying to cage him, 'some were so sweet I barely got free'. There's no intro, and it's more or less divided into two parts. The first one is again almost a ballad, with gloriously restrained guitar, piano and organ most prominent. Halfway through, the drummer is set free, and it all catches fire. Seger works himself up into a frenzy on vocals, matched by Pete Carr on a glorious bit of guitar soloing. Then, for the last 30 seconds, the backing on the ending of the song reverts to restraint, and the effect is magical. It's one of those songs that needs to be listened to several times in order to appreciate just how well it is put together.

'Momma' 3:21
Backing band: Muscle Shoals Rhythm Section
Another ballad – or should that be power ballad? Seger pours his heart out in a tribute to his mother, Charlotte, a single parent to him and his elder brother after Mr Seger Sr. left – Seger was the baby, the 'quiet other'. It was a strict upbringing, he recalls in the lyrics. He was scolded when he misbehaved, but she never told him a lie – and she never promised him the sky, either. As in 'Travelin' Man', there are peaks and troughs when Seger sings softly or alternatively goes for the soulful passion. The musicians excel themselves, organ and piano holding back and complementing each other, sometimes the organ and guitar solo breaking free and building up to a crescendo before receding back into the background. In just over three minutes, it's a wonderful balance of light and shade.

Three years later, he opened up to Steve Morse of the *Boston Globe*:

> A lot of people thought that song was a bunch of mush, but too bad. My mother had just had a heart attack, and I was sort of trying to bring her out of it. She was worried about life in general, about making it much further. But that song really helped bring her out, so I will take the criticisms. Screw them. The song made her happy.

It made Mrs Seger happy and indeed helped her make it much further. She lived for another 13 years.

'Nutbush City Limits' (Tina Turner) 3:52

Backing band: The Silver Bullet Band

Just as Bob Seger and The Last Heard had covered the first Ike and Tina Turner epic, he and The Silver Bullet Band had to do the same with the second. Bearing in mind what a good reputation they were getting as a live group, one almost wishes that they'd done as they had on the *Mongrel* album and recorded this one in concert as well. (Record buyers only had to wait for a few months for that.) This studio version still finds them firing on all cylinders, even if they felt the need to wrap it up in a little less than four minutes. Abbott's guitar growls appropriately, and Cartmell puts in some fine work on saxophone, even though he could have perhaps been a little higher in the mix. Even so, the result is still a real blast, and perfectly placed on the original vinyl, sandwiched between two mellow tunes on either side.

One can't help feeling that Capitol missed a trick. Nine years later, they signed Tina Turner, long since split from Ike both professionally and personally, as a soloist. In doing so, they turned her from an almost has-been into a global megastar until her retirement due to ill-health. She was also teamed up for successful one-off duets on other labels with Eric Clapton, Bryan Adams and Rod Stewart. Seger similarly recorded a few numbers with other female singers in later years, and both were surely the greatest vocalists with the company at that time. Did anybody ever consider a Bob and Tina duet as well?

'Sailing Nights' 3:16

Backing band: Muscle Shoals Rhythm Section

When is a ballad perhaps not strictly a ballad? This slow song and its structure, with its metaphors of travelling on the waters – 'I can see there's no use sailing among ships I've known before' – and the music, to say nothing of the often dominant organ and Seger's Gary Brookerish vocals, sounds remarkably like Procol Harum. That's not intended as disrespect, but it captures a similar sense of classics-tinged rock with a hint of soul.

'Fine Memory' 2:58

Backing band: Muscle Shoals Rhythm Section

The album ends on a short, sweet and beautifully simple three minutes of romance. After one night of making love, the narrator leaves, driving away as the sky is getting light, and takes away 'such a fine memory'. Reduced to a cold word-for-word appraisal may not do it justice, but it's a very appealing listen as Seger picks at the strings of his acoustic guitar, discreetly supplemented by organ and bass.

Night Moves (1976)

Personnel:
Bob Seger: lead vocals, guitar, piano
The Silver Bullet Band:
Drew Abbott: lead guitar, backing vocals
Alto Reed (formerly known as Tom Cartmell): tenor, alto and baritone saxes, flute
Robyn Robbins: piano, organ
Chris Campbell: bass, backing vocals
Charlie Martin: drums, tambourine, backing vocals
The Muscle Shoals Rhythm Section:
Pete Carr: lead, rhythm and acoustic guitars
Barry Beckett: piano, organ, Arp, clavinet, melodica
David Hood: bass
Roger Hawkins: drums, tambourine, maracas, congas, timpani drum
Jimmy Johnson: rhythm guitar
Additional musicians:
Jerry Luck: accordion
Joe Miquelon: guitar
Doug Riley: piano, organ
Sharon Lee Williams, Rhonda Silver, Laurel Ward: backing vocals
Produced by Punch Andrews and Bob Seger; Bob Seger and M.S.R.S.; Jack Richardson and Bob Seger
Recorded at Muscle Shoals Sound Studios, Alabama; Pampa Sound Studios, Detroit; Nimbus Nine Studios, Toronto
Release date: October 1976
Highest chart positions: UK: did not chart, US: 8
Certification: 6x Platinum
Running time: 36:50

Like the in-concert *'Live' Bullet* that preceded it, this also proved to be another career record. While making it, Seger said he hoped 'that the *Night Moves* album would be the one, and by God, that was the one. We went from station wagons to jets after that album came out. We never did a bus tour, we never were in-between.'

The release of a massively successful live album and then a studio album within a few months proved a real game-changer for singer and band, as well as instantly affirming the label's faith in re-signing an act they had previously let go. *Night Moves* spawned two top 40 singles, one of them top 10, and was his first album to go Platinum (one million units) – later six times Platinum. It gave him the confidence to feel he could vary his musical palate.

> I'd like to do softer stuff, I really would, but I'm scared. Our show is frenetic and meant to be hard rock, and that's fun, but 'Night Moves' is such a change. I'm scared because I don't know if I can sing well enough to do soft

> stuff. I do write about 60% ballads. They are more fun and easier to write because you can be more melancholy and dramatic in a ballad, say things slower.

By this time, he was at the top of his game. Expectations were high, and he was not only now a major name in his home country, but the word was spreading across Europe as well. In Britain, John Peel had been featuring his music on the Radio 1 evening show from time to time since *Smokin' O.P.'s*, and played several tracks from *Night Moves* shortly after release. On reviewing one of Seger's singles in *NME* a few years later, he mentioned having once had a tour jacket with Bob's name on, and gave it to his mother. If anybody should ever see a woman in her 70s walking round Notting Hill in such a garment, he said, it was almost certainly her.

'Rock And Roll Never Forgets' 3:52
Backing band: The Silver Bullet Band
Produced by Punch Andrews and Bob Seger
There's nothing like a really exuberant start to an album. You can't help but applaud the man's honesty when he lays it on the line in the first verse of a song that he wrote after attending a high school reunion. He's a little bit older and a lot less bold than he used to be, so now he stops and thinks about his dignity. Hell, sweet 16's now 31 (yes, he was 31 at the time), and he may be getting older, feeling weary when his day's work is done, but nothing will prevent him from connecting with the rock 'n' roll music of his youth that he loves and is part of his DNA. It's off to the concert or the local bar where 'the rafters will be ringing 'cause the beat's so strong'. Over a genuine full force ten piledriver of a song, he throws himself into a defiant endorsement of eternal youth in music. As he sings in the last verse, 'Well all Chuck's children are out there playing his licks, get into your kicks'. The whole thing ends in a blaze of glory with Drew's guitar and Reed's sax trying to outshine each other on the instrumental break as it fades, and it's a dead heat. As Seger would say later, the effect was 'just slammin'. When we play that song live people go nuts.'

The third single from the album on both sides of the Atlantic, it never quite achieved its due as a hit on its own, just peaking at a modest number 41 on its home ground.

'Night Moves' 5:25
Backing band: The Silver Bullet Band
Produced by Jack Richardson and Bob Seger
The title track, from initial writing to recording, took around six months to complete. 'I wrote my brains out', Seger commented later. A cocktail of influences helped to inspire and shape it, notably the coming-of-age movie *American Graffiti*, and the story and general writing style of Kris Kristofferson's 'Me And Bobby McGee', a song he had always loved. His

intention was to capture what he called the 'freedom and looseness' of adolescence, the feeling of 'youthful passion and the danger of letting that slip away.' For him, it was in a sense 'the easiest song in the world to write but the hardest song to finish.' It took him six months to complete, and he had the first two verses, but lacked inspiration to finish it until he heard Bruce Springsteen's 'Jungleland' and had the idea of including two bridges.

To some extent, it's autobiographical, about a young couple losing their virginity in the back seat of a Chevy. He is recalling the carefree days of being part of a group of friends who would take part in 'grassers', or parties on summer evenings where they would gather to dance – this being another, perhaps more innocent, explanation of 'night moves' than the more obvious one. At one of these events, the 19-year-old Bob met a dark-haired Italian girl whose boyfriend was on military service. They had a brief affair before her soldier love interest came home and married a little later, leaving him desolate. Evidently smitten, he admitted he had written several songs to try to impress her. In the lyrics, he mentions her, the cornfields where the woods got heavy, how they were young, restless and bored, trying to lose the awkward teenage blues – all the confused feelings of late adulthood. Many years later, he wakes one night after a clap of thunder, his mind goes back to those times and he starts humming a song from 1962 – 'Be My Baby' by The Ronettes, apparently (which was actually 1963).

There was also a third possible meaning to the title. The following year, he told *Mix* that he liked it because it was two-edged. (Only two?) 'It had a duality to it, our 'night moves' with girls and 'ain't it funny how the night moves' – what you remember as you're getting older.' Six years later, he told Timothy White of *Crawdaddy* that when he wrote it, he was also thinking about 'the whole aura of nighttime, the 4.00 in the morning moment when you assess yourself, check your weaknesses.'

Even the seasons mentioned in the lyrics had two meanings. 'And it was summertime, sweet summertime, summertime' is not just the time of the year, but also that season of his life as well. In the last verse, he muses, 'With autumn closing in', referring to the autumn of his life as he gets to his 30s and beyond.

It was the last song to be finished and recorded for the album. Four tracks had been completed at Alabama and Detroit, and they needed one more. Andrews booked three days at Nimbys Nie Studios, Toronto, with Jack Nicholson, best known for producing The Guess Who, and they completed three more numbers, a cover version of The Supremes' 'My World Is Empty Without You' and two written by Seger. One of these was probably 'Suicide Streets'. He told John Morthland of *Creem* that nobody in the band was very enthusiastic about it.

> It was about crime in the streets, sort of a Springsteen-ish thing, but with real ominous lyrics. And I was gonna name the album after it; the album

> would have a concept about nightlife in general. When nobody liked that song, it sort of blew the whole thing away, and I was back to square one. I thought 'Night Moves' made a better title anyway, though I still wanted 'Suicide Streets' on the LP. Then I got to thinking that maybe 'Suicide Streets' was a little too down. Frankly, I was afraid people might have thought I was writing about Detroit, which I wasn't.

As none of these extra songs seemed satisfactory, two of the band returned to Detroit. Chris Campbell and drummer Charlie Martin stayed behind, and Richardson recruited local session musicians Joe Miquelon on guitar and Doug Riley on piano and organ. Seger had almost finished writing 'Night Moves' but felt it needed a little work.

Between them, plus three female backing vocalists, the song was completed; according to Richardson, it 'came together in the studio', while he and Seger came up with the extra 'sound of thunder' bridge idea. Paul Cotton of Poco was also brought in to play lead guitar; most of his contribution was erased, and he was not credited on the album sleeve, although a few of his notes can be heard just before the last verse.

Although it had been a complicated song for Seger to complete, it was recorded in less than ten takes. The whole arrangement is a masterclass in subtlety. His folksy three-chord strummed intro on acoustic guitar sets the scene, then he starts singing the first verse, joined by bass and gentle drums, with piano on the chorus; momentum gradually builds up on the second verse with backing vocals, and organ on the next chorus, followed by a bridge, and a brief halt. Then comes the 'sound of thunder' bridge, with just his vocal and simple acoustic guitar for almost a minute, and another halt. Back comes the intro, a few seconds of vocal, then the piano signals a return for the whole ensemble of organ, bass, drums and backing vocals for the last 90 seconds, with Seger singing his heart out until they all reach a tidy finish.

Prior to the session, he had played an embryonic version on piano to Richardson in his office, wondering whether it was good enough. Richardson liked it but agreed it was not quite there. At one point, they were still at the studio in Toronto at 2 am, frustrated as they were trying to come up with something that sounded like a single and not really getting anywhere. Then, he later recalled, 'I pulled out this song.' Once everybody heard the finished results, they knew they had something special. Even Seger himself, who admitted he was never really one for choosing singles and was happy to leave such decisions to the company, agreed with them. Shortly afterwards, Bruce Wendell, one of the Capitol promotion staff, told him it was a 'career record' and warned him it was 'a song that you're gonna have to play for the rest of your life.'

The label insisted that it would be the title track of the next album and the first single, albeit shortened by two minutes, with a truncated intro, the 'sound of thunder' bridge omitted and an early fadeout. The single followed the album release by a few weeks, and after a three-month climb, peaked at number four in the US for two weeks. In the UK, it had respectable airplay, although without charting, until it became the second CD single off *Greatest Hits* 18 years later and belatedly made number 45. Over the years, it has regularly topped music journalists' polls as Seger's best song of all time.

Its creator evidently shared their views. A few years later, he told Timothy White of *Musician Player & Listener*, 'I don't know if I'll ever write one as good as that again. But I must say that 'Night Moves' is my favorite song, overall. I milked 'Night Moves' a little bit after that with 'Brave Strangers' and 'Against The Wind', but material of that nature became a problem for me. I kept trying to out-write 'Night Moves', and finally said, 'No more. I'm not gonna try to out-write it."

One small glitch marred proceedings. When the single charted, Nicholson was annoyed to notice that on the label, Seger and Andrews had been named as co-producers, and considered taking legal action. It was presumably an oversight, as he and Seger had been jointly credited on the album sleeve (if not the album label), although it has been said that he was the sole producer of the track.

'The Fire Down Below' 4:28

Backing band: The Silver Bullet Band

Produced by Punch Andrews and Bob Seger

A song title like that could have any number of meanings. It could refer to eternal fire and brimstone in hell; a longing for deep personal connection; or plain, undisguised carnal lust. This time, it's the latter – or more specifically, customers in the red light district. 'Here come the men faces hidden from the light', the rich, the poor, the bankers, lawyers, cops, men with only one thing in common – 'they got the fire down below'. In an interview shortly after the album's release, Seger said that for members of a rock band, after playing a show, the adrenaline is flowing; they generally spend two or three hours wide awake from midnight after leaving the concert hall to go out, and notice plenty of nightlife action in the big cities. 'That song comes from personal observation.'

Those who remember Frankie Miller's 'Ain't Got No Money' from his album *The Rock* (1975) might detect some resemblance. Seger commented several times that he was a big fan of Miller, thinking they were both very similar in the way they approached rock 'n' roll. He also revealed that Don Henley and Glenn Frey were as well, and they all wanted to work together, but there was never enough time. When he heard 'Money', he liked 'that swampy middle-rock thing'. Although he was partly inspired by Miller when he wrote this song, band-wise, he had in mind another song, 'Rattlesnake Shake' by the original Peter Green-led Fleetwood Mac. More on this will come in the next chapter.

Robyn Robbins's mean, lean piano and a splendid, snarling bluesy guitar from Drew hold it all together tightly, and there's a neat little false ending when Seger counts the band back in for a few more bars before the proper finish.

'Sunburst' 5:13

Backing band: The Silver Bullet Band

Produced by Punch Andrews and Bob Seger

This is probably the most enigmatic lyric on the album. We can safely say that this one isn't written from experience, but is perhaps based on a legendary war leader from some bygone age. He enters the arena and flashes a weapon before his legions as the fires begin to rage. It begins gently enough with a descending four-chord sequence on piano (did anyone say ELO's '10538 Overture'?) to introduce the first two verses, ending in a dramatic call to 'Bring on the night!' At this point, guitar, bass and drums all explode, and it rocks like fury for the next 90 seconds. Then it returns calmly to the opening piano chords, with Reed adding not sax this time, but a gentle flute, as the concluding verse leads us to the hero's escape, with a final dramatic chord bringing the curtain down.

'Sunspot Baby' 4:38

Backing band: The Muscle Shoals Rhythm Section

Produced by Bob Seger and M.S.R.S.

Back to one of rock 'n' roll's tried and tested themes, and what better way to do it than just three chords on rhythm guitar, reminiscent of T. Rex at their peak, a nice 'n' dirty guitar solo that brings to mind the likes of Ronnie Wood and barrelhouse piano holding it all together. The lyric is about a deceiving young woman who charges up a fortune on his credit card, leaving him stranded with a false address. In the last line, he vows he will catch up with her. It would have been perfect for The Faces had they not split a year earlier.

'Mainstreet' 3:43

Backing band: The Muscle Shoals Rhythm Section

Produced by Bob Seger and M.S.R.S.

As with the album's title track, there is plenty of reminiscing here as Seger thinks back to his adolescence, 'the discovery, the total naïveté and fresh–faced openness'.

The setting is a club in Ann Street, just off Main Street in Ann Arbor, Michigan. In his high school days, a blues band from Chicago would be playing there on weekends. He could stand outside and watch people dancing, and sometimes there would be a particularly attractive girl in the window, as the lyrics say: 'through the long, lonely nights she filled my sleep, her body softly swaying to that smoky beat'. He always called the experience 'sort of an entire awakening of my life; before that, I was kind of a quiet, lonesome kid.' She was unattainable, and he could only admire her from afar as she walked back alone after closing time, down on Main Street. But he still thinks about her: 'When I'm feeling lonely and beat, drift back in time'.

Pete Carr's guitar provides not only a gorgeous intro but a few connecting phrases and a break over a relaxed backdrop of piano, Hammond organ and guitar. The title track of the album is sheer beauty, but this runs it very close.

At the time and also retrospectively, journalists praised this ode to the romantic backstreets of hope and despair, comparing it to Van Morrison at his most introspective. There were comparisons with Bruce Springsteen, not always favorable either, with *New Musical Express* opining that 'leaning heavily on anyone so personally stylized as that has got to qualify as an error of judgment.' Yet Seger was always honest about his influences and freely admitted that his music owed much to the younger man, who had such an effect on his songwriting. Seeing him at a show in 1975 and listening to *Born To Run* had given him an incentive to complete songs for the partly-written album, even if it meant locking himself away in a room for two weeks to see the job through.

Moreover, he recognized a kindred spirit: 'Something signaled that I wasn't alone anymore; there's someone else who thinks as I think. What I really gleaned from Bruce was passion – just tremendous passion in his lyrics. You get that from Henley and Dylan, too.' Down the years, fans and journalists alike would often debate among themselves who was superior – the one from Detroit or the one from New Jersey. Bob Dylan once opined on his *Theme Time Radio Hour* show that 'A lot of people call Bob Seger a poor man's Bruce Springsteen, but personally I always thought Bruce was the rich man's Bob Seger.'

The second single from the album, 'Mainstreet' peaked at a respectable number 24 in the US, and number one in Canada.

'Come To Poppa' (Earl Randle, Willie Mitchell) 3:11
Backing band: The Muscle Shoals Rhythm Section
Produced by Bob Seger and M.S.R.S.
Originally recorded a year earlier by Ann Peebles as 'Come To Mama', this lets Seger indulge his passion for the odd helping of funky soul, to say nothing of giving Drew free rein on wah-wah guitar. It's nothing groundbreaking, but an enjoyable three minutes or so. There have been subsequent cover versions by Etta James, Shaun Murphy – who sang backing vocals on the *Beautiful Loser* album under the alias of Stoney (both recordings renamed 'Come To Mama') – and Willy DeVille.

'Ship Of Fools' 3:24
Backing band: The Muscle Shoals Rhythm Section
Produced by Bob Seger and M.S.R.S.
Enter Bob Seger, the mellow country rock singer, turning to a genre he would visit more and more on future albums. This is a story song of a shipwreck, with all hands on deck lost beneath the waves except himself. Drew's gently picked lead guitar and some silvery accordion fills from session musician Jerry Luck fit this song like a glove.

'Mary Lou' (Young Jessie, Sam Ling) 2:56
Backing band: The Silver Bullet Band
Produced by Punch Andrews and Bob Seger
Back to vintage rock 'n' roll for the last track, with a song first recorded by Ronnie Hawkins in 1959. Mary Lou is another Sunspot Baby, who does a disappearing act with her unlucky lover's Cadillac and diamond ring. This shuffle is heavy on the drum, with call and response vocals from Abbott, Campbell and Martin, and a fun way to finish what has always been regarded as one of Seger's classic albums – if not the ultimate classic one.

Stranger In Town (1978)

Personnel:
Bob Seger: lead vocals, guitar, piano
The Silver Bullet Band:
Drew Abbott: lead guitar
Robyn Robbins: keyboards
Alto Reed: horns
Chris Campbell: bass
David Teegarden: drums, tambourine
The Muscle Shoals Rhythm Section:
Pete Carr: lead guitar
Jimmy Johnson: rhythm guitar
David Hood: bass
Roger Hawkins: drums, percussion
Additional musicians:
Ken Bell, Glenn Frey, Don Felder, Howie McDonald: guitar
Bill Payne: piano, organ
Doug Riley, Randy McCormick: piano
Brandye, Stanley Carter, James Lavell Easley, Venetta Fields, George Jackson, Clydie King, Shirley Matthews, Julie Waters, Luther Waters, Maxine Waters, Oren Waters: backing vocals
Produced by Punch Andrews and Bob Seger
Recorded at Criteria Sound Studios, Miami; Muscle Shoals Sound Studios, Alabama; Cherokee Studios, Los Angeles; Capitol Records Studios, Hollywood; Sound Suite Studios, Detroit
Release date: May 1978
Highest chart positions: UK: 31, US: 4
Certification: 6x Platinum (US), Gold (UK)
Running time: 39:28

The title of *Stranger In Town* was said to have been inspired by one of Del Shannon's last major hits, although some say that it also hinted at a sense of Seger's discomfort with his newfound fame. Later, it emerged that he had recorded a song of that name, but rejected it as he thought sales of the record might suffer because there could be confusion with this and Billy Joel's new work, *The Stranger*. [See 'Unreleased songs' below].

It was recorded across five studios, with seven different engineers, over 25 different musicians and backing vocalists and also a string section. Sometimes his own fiercest critic, he told Steve Morse of the *Boston Globe* that he felt the new album lacked the songwriting peaks of *Night Moves,* but was more consistent. It proved far more successful as well. Seger and the band had played a series of six well-received arena dates in Britain in October 1977, and after a show at the Palace Theatre, Manchester, Pete Makowski wrote in *Sounds* that Seger 'should be (and will be) up there with the kingpins.' They reaped the dividend this time when *Stranger In Town* broke them through into the singles and album charts, and initial sales were boosted a little later by limited pressings on silver vinyl and, for the album only, picture disc.

Since *Night Moves*, there had been one sad but unavoidable alteration to The Silver Bullet Band lineup. In 1977, drummer Charlie Martin was involved in a severe car accident that left him paralyzed from the waist down, and David Teegarden rejoined.

Press reaction to the album was uniformly favorable. One of the most positive comments came from *Rolling Stone*, in which Dave Marsh called it 'a perfect balance of high energy rock and moving personal ballad.'

'Hollywood Nights' 4:59

Backing Band: The Silver Bullet Band

The opening track of the album was one of the last songs to be completed. He had gone to Los Angeles for the final stage of working on it. While he was there, he rented a house in the Hollywood Hills, with a first-class view of the city's bright lights. This gave the album its name and, at the same time, inspired a song that would become one of his classics. The result, he said later, was the closest he ever had to a song coming to him in a dream. Normally, he had a guitar or a keyboard nearby. It was rare for him to have something come into his head while he was driving, but this one did. The lines, 'Hollywood nights, Hollywood Hills, above all the lights, Hollywood nights', entered his head. So he immediately turned round, drove home and he sang this to himself, thinking: 'Don't forget it, don't forget it! Don't turn on the radio!' As soon as he got back, he sang it into a small cassette recorder.

Also at the house was a recent issue of *Time* magazine with a picture of model Cheryl Tiegs on the cover. From this came the idea of a story about an innocent young man from the Midwest who comes to Hollywood, and meets his ideal girl, who 'had been born with a face that would let her get her way'. They embark on a brief series of whirlwind adventures, and he loses all control. Sadly for him, it comes to a sudden end one morning when he wakes up alone and finds himself looking over the Hollywood Hills, wondering if he can ever go home. The Sunspot Baby of the previous album has found another unsuspecting victim.

The result is nothing short of a sonic masterpiece. It's a helter skelter, dizzying fairground of a song, lyrically and musically, and even more so when we realize that it's all done on three chords, E, A and D, throughout those five minutes. Vocally and instrumentally, it scores five out of five on all fronts, perhaps most of all with that pattern of galloping drums. Teegarden achieved it by recording one take on one set of drums, and then went to another set to overdub an entirely different pattern over the top. Add to that Chris Campbell's superlative runs of bass notes, not to mention a brief snatch of what sounds like ersatz disco on the instrument, and you have an astonishing rhythm section. Little Feat's Bill Payne does an equally fine job with the piano and shimmering organ fills, as do the Waters siblings (Julia, Maxine, Luther and Oren) on backing vocals. When he had finished, he asked for a tape to listen to on his way home. The next day, he rang Seger to tell him that while he'd been listening, he looked at the dashboard and found he had been driving 100 m.p.h. on the freeway. Backing vocals add the same soulful touch that had so enhanced 'Night Moves'.

The second single from the album, not for the first time unnecessarily edited by two minutes, it reached number 12 in the US. In the UK, the full album version on black (and a limited pressing on silver) vinyl gave him his long-overdue chart debut at number 42. British labels were more prepared to release the full versions of album tracks on singles and issue an edit on promotional copies than their American counterparts, who found that radio resistance to long 45s was greater. A live version from *Nine Tonight* in 1981 surfaced in the UK as a single and charted at number 49, while a reissue of the original version in 1995, this time only on CD, reached number 52.

'Still The Same' 3:18
Backing band: The Silver Bullet Band
The first track to be released as a single was a more restrained mid-tempo song about a compulsive gambler who always seems a step ahead. Seger was often asked if it was referring to anybody in particular, and he always replied that it was an amalgamation of different characters, all 'Type A overachievers' whom he had met in Hollywood. He had his reservations about such people: 'They're just very charismatic, but they have tremendous faults, but part of the appeal is the charisma.' For once, there is no electric guitar, just Seger playing acoustic and piano, plus the rhythm section, keyboards and backing vocals. A number four hit at home, it never charted in the UK, although it was his first single to receive regular BBC Radio 1 daytime airplay.

In 2006, Rod Stewart included it on one of his cover version albums, *Still The Same: Great Rock Classics Of Our Time*, a number one US album and top five in the UK.

'Old Time Rock And Roll' (George Jackson, Thomas Earl Jones III; Seger [uncredited]) 3:14
Backing band: The Muscle Shoals Rhythm Section
Who really wrote this song? As someone once said, 'recollections may vary'. The official version is that Jackson and Jones, part of the Muscle Shoals Rhythm Section (although they weren't part of the team that played on Seger's records), created it and gave him a demo while he was recording the album, and he decided to include it after rewriting some of the lyrics. According to him, all he kept from the original were the lines:

Old time rock 'n' roll,
That kind of music just soothes the soul,

I reminisce about the days of old
With that old time rock 'n' roll

He insisted that, among other lines, he was also responsible for:

Don't try to take me to a disco,
You'll never even get me out on the floor,
In ten minutes I'll be late for the door,
I like that old time rock 'n' roll

This swipe at his least-favored genre was ahead of its time and has gone down in history. The 'disco sucks' battle cry didn't come until the following year, and when *Stranger In Town* was released, the *Saturday Night Fever* soundtrack album was wedged firmly atop the US charts – from January to July 1978. Short of flying to the moon, there was no escaping disco. Nobody has owned up to borrowing/lifting the Chuck Berry-penned line, 'Won't go to hear 'em play a tango'.

George Stephenson of Malaco Records worked regularly with George Jackson, who had died in 2013. He disputed the rewriting issue, saying that it was genuinely Jackson and Jones's song, and he had the original tapes to prove his case. Seger had more or less finished his recording at Muscle Shoals, asked them if they had any songs that he could consider for future albums and disputed Stephenson's claims. Bassist David Hood, who played on the track, agreed with Seger.

The Silver Bullet Band weren't initially keen on the song, so Seger and Andrews bought the original demo, erased the vocals and the singer added his own to the backing track. Despite asserting he was responsible for most of the lyrics, he waived any credit, saying that nobody was going to like it and he just wanted to get the record finished. He had no idea just how popular it would become, and later he admitted that his decision was the dumbest thing he had ever done, as he thus had no claim to either the composing royalties or any control over subsequent use in movies and commercials. It would be the fourth US single from the album in the summer of 1979, reaching number 28, though only a B-side in the UK. After being included in the 1983 movie *Risky Business,* with Tom Cruise's soon-to-be iconic scene lip-synching and dancing to it in his underwear, it was reissued and sold sufficiently to reach number 48 in the US. The song charted years later in the UK, when Status Quo took it to number 78 in 2001.

Appropriately for a late 1970s song celebrating the spirit of a genre that ruled supreme some two decades earlier and had never gone out of fashion, it's a simple, direct song both lyrically and musically. It drives its message home in just three minutes, its verses interwoven with solos from guitar and sax, with a steady backbone of guitars, piano, drums and bass. According to a survey by

Bob Seger performing on stage in the late 1970s, on the threshold of full international success after *Night Moves*. (*Alamy*)

Left: Bob Seger and The System's debut album, originally titled *Tales Of Lucy Blue*, was renamed *Ramblin' Gamblin' Man* at Capitol's insistence after the top 20 US hit single. (*Capitol/Universal Music*)

Right: The group's second album, *Noah*, on which Seger's dissatisfaction with Tom Neme joining almost led to him leaving the music business altogether. (*Capitol/Universal Music*)

Left: Don't be fooled by the sleeve design. *Mongrel* is generally regarded as Seger's hardest-rocking set ever. (*Capitol/Universal Music*)

Right: *Brand New Morning* – no band, no overdubs, just one man, his voice, acoustic guitar and piano, on a completely solo effort. (*Capitol/Universal Music*)

Left: A return to the full band format on *Smokin' O.P.'s* resulted in what was mostly a 'smokin'' set of other people's songs, including Leon Russell, Chuck Berry, Tim Hardin and others. (*Capitol/Universal Music*)

Right: Unhappy with the 'awful mix' and the sound of his voice on this album, Seger would never allow a reissue of *Back In '72*, despite the presence of classics like 'Turn The Page' and 'Rosalie'. (*Palladium/Warner Bros*)

Above: Bob Seger and The Last Heard, 1966. L-R: Dan Honaker (bass), Seger (at front) (vocal, guitar, organ), Pep Perrine (drums), Carl Legassa (guitar). (*Getty Images*)
Below: Seger at his photographer Tom Weschler's apartment in Birmingham, Alabama, 1972, while trying to take a picture of Tom taking a picture of him – so the story goes. (*Tom Weschler*)

Above: The Bob Seger System, 1970. L-R: Seger, Honaker, Dan Watson (organ, piano), Perrine. (*Tom Weschler*)

Right: A moment of relaxation for manager Edward 'Punch' Andrews and Seger at Ann Arbor, 1970. (*Tom Weschler*)

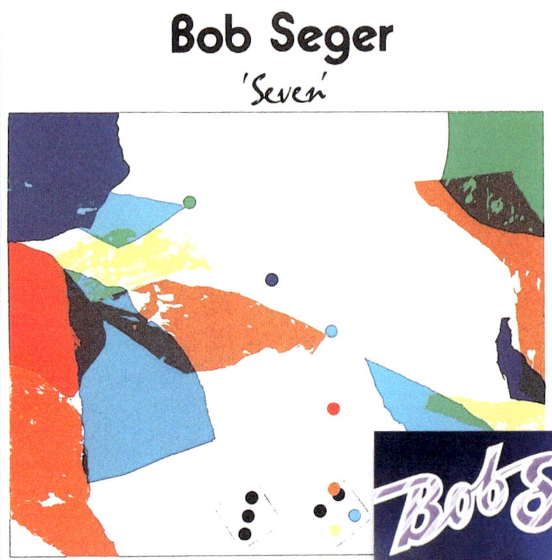

Left: Seger's second completely self-composed album, *Seven*, is mostly full-tilt rock 'n' roll, kicking off with the much-covered 'Get Out Of Denver'. (*Palladium/Warner Bros*)

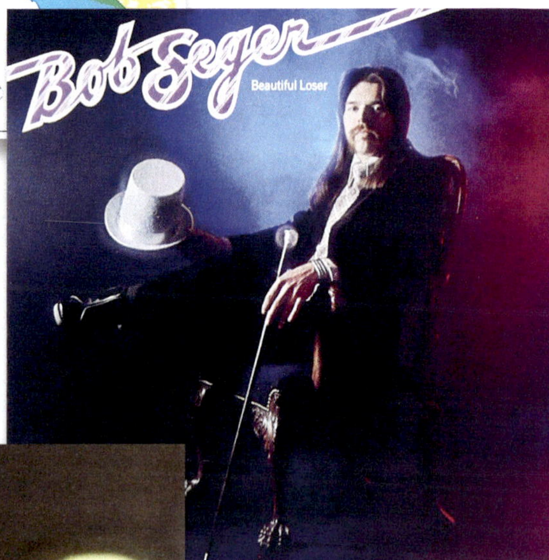

Right: Rejected by Warner Bros, the relatively introspective *Beautiful Loser* marked Seger's return to Capitol, the title track inspired by the name of a Leonard Cohen novel. (*Capitol/ Universal Music*)

Left: 'We went from station wagons to jets after that album came out', Seger said. *Night Moves* went six times platinum in the US and is still regarded as his best. (*Capitol/ Universal Music*)

Right: A UK press ad where, for once, the praise was justified. *Cash Box*'s review noted: '[Seger] has become much wiser, realising that good production values and screaming rock 'n' roll are not mutually exclusive.' (*Capitol/Universal Music*)

Left: A poster for the opening dates of the 1977 US tour at Cobo Arena, Detroit, where they had recorded *Live Bullet* 16 months earlier.

Left: Seger's international breakthrough album, particularly in the UK, where *Stranger In Town* went top 40 and spawned two top 50 singles, 'Hollywood Nights' and 'We've Got Tonite'. (*Capitol/Universal Music*)

Right: Seger admitted that with *Against The Wind*, they 'dropped away a little bit from rockiness', and it was their first US number one album, staying there for six weeks. (*Capitol/Universal Music*)

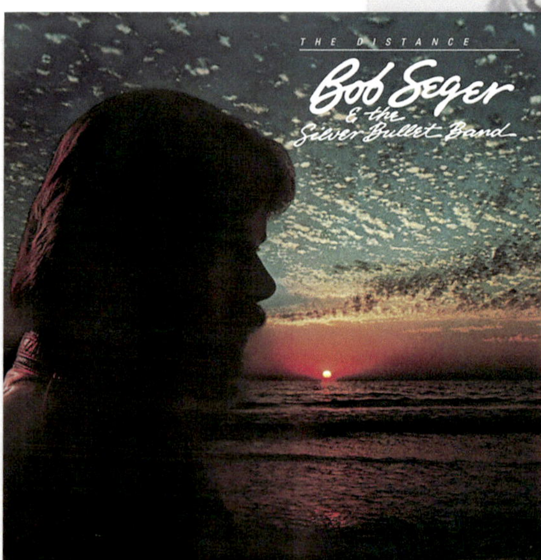

Left: Now writing and recording so prolifically, Seger initially considered making *The Distance* a double album, an idea he dropped as it would be priced too expensively for fans. (*Capitol/Universal Music*)

Above: Seger and The Silver Bullet Band, 1977. L-R: Seger, Drew Abbott (guitar), Chris Campbell (bass), Robyn Robbins (keyboards), Alto Reed (sax), Charlie Martin (drums). (*Malcolm Clarke/Keystone/Getty Images*)
Below: Seger on stage, 1977, the year that saw them play a 65-date US tour as well as six shows in the UK, three in Germany and two in France.

Above: Seger and Bruce Springsteen at Pine Knob Theatre, September 1978. The latter played the Masonic Auditorium the previous night, then came to Seger's gig and met him afterwards. (*Tom Weschler*)
Below: Seger and 'the bullets' at the end of a show, Pine Knob Theatre, Clarkston, Michigan, July 1977. (*Tom Weschler*)

Right: Sales of *Stranger In Town* in the UK were boosted by limited pressings on silver vinyl and also picture disc. (*Capitol/ Universal Music*)

Left: The 1977 tour logo used on official T-shirts. (*Kurt's Kustom Promotions*)

Left: A more mature Seger, who said of *Like A Rock*: 'I'm sure it doesn't mean much to someone who's 20, but I gotta write what I know about.' (*Capitol/Universal Music*)

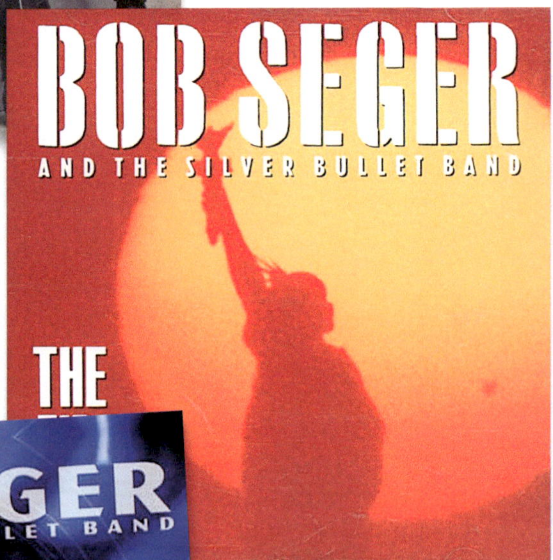

Right: According to one of the co-producers, Don Was, listeners would find on *The Fire Inside* that 'there's a lot of not typical Seger material.' (*Capitol/Universal Music*)

Left: Created by graphic designer Norman Moore, the eye on the cover of *It's A Mystery* is intended as an 'all-seeing' artistic symbol meant to represent universal themes of wisdom, perception and the unknown. (*Capitol/Universal Music*)

Right: Released after an 11-year hiatus and a definite return to form, *Face The Promise* was Seger's first top-five album since *Like A Rock*, and the only one so far unissued on vinyl. (*Capitol/Universal Music*)

Left: *Ride Out* is a thoughtful album, with several lyrics reflecting his views on mortality, gun culture, climate change and the concerns of a man wondering what kind of world his children will face. (*Capitol/Universal Music*)

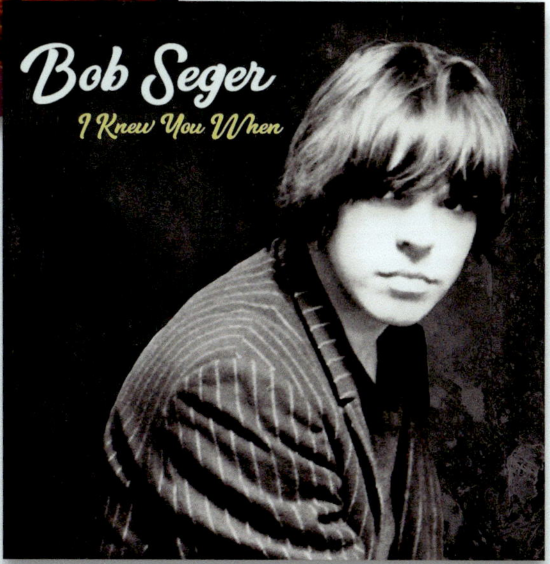

Right: *I Knew You When* is the last of Seger's 18 studio albums, with a cover photo of him aged 21 and a title track dedicated to his friend, the recently deceased Glenn Frey. (*Capitol/Universal Music*)

Left: A UK press ad for Seger's January 1983 single 'Shame On The Moon', which failed in Britain but reached number two in the US.

Below: Seger and The Silver Bullet Band, now increasingly augmented with session musicians, c.1986-88. L-R: Alto Reed (sax), Craig Frost (keyboards), Seger, Chris Campbell (bass). (*Getty Images*)

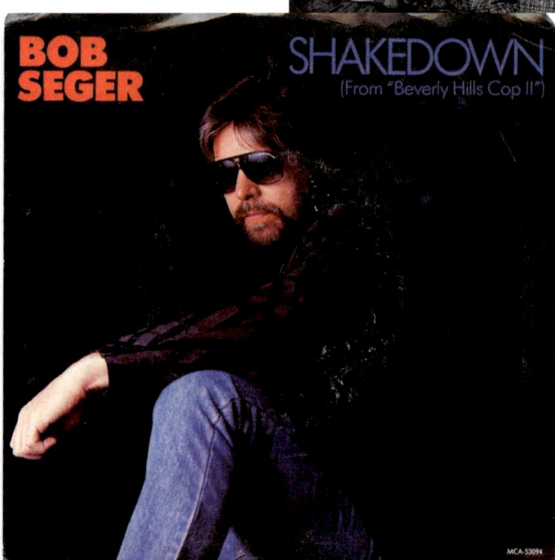

Left: 'Shakedown', from the *Beverly Hills Cop II* soundtrack, Seger's only number one single in the US, co-written with Harold Faltermeyer and Keith Forsey. (*MCA/Universal*)

Right: A poster for the North American tour 2006-7. By this time, Seger was spending less time on the road and more with his family.

Left: Seger at the Fargodome, Fargo, North Dakota, March 2013, when he was joined onstage by Kid Rock for four encores. (*Adam Freese, Wikimedia CreativeCommons*)

Left: The long-unavailable Bob Seger and The Last Heard mid-1960s singles eventually appeared on the CD and vinyl compilation *Heavy Music* in 2018. (*ABKCO/Universal Music*)

Right: The in-concert double album *Live Bullet*, recorded in September 1975, was released the following year and finally launched Seger as a major name in the US. (*Capitol/Universal Music*)

Newsweek and the Amusement and Music Operations Association published by *Los Angeles Times* in March 1990, in a list of the top ten greatest jukebox hits of all time, it was placed ninth, the only non-1950s or 1960s single on the list. What might have been regarded at the time by its writers as a simple throwaway has struck a chord with many for its unrepentant nostalgia and yearning for a long-gone age when music and times were simpler.

'Till It Shines' 3:50
Backing band: The Muscle Shoals Rhythm Section
Laid-back, almost a folk ballad but not quite, this starts off with gently-strummed acoustic guitar, shining organ and mellow electric guitar a little way in. It's a philosophical, gently optimistic lyric, looking forward to an escape to better times and better places: 'storm the walls around this prison, take me out among the rustling pines'. The drums add some more muscle, and Glenn Frey contributes a guitar solo towards the end. It's as good an example as any of Seger's skill as an arranger, opening a song gently and gradually building it up musically, layer by layer. It was released as the fourth UK single but never charted.

A review by Simon Frith in *Melody Maker* scathingly called it 'effortlessly executed compact rock that rolls along like an expensive car. Fittingly, Seger throws out one carefully-planned line after another, platitudes disguised as hard-bitten philosophy for Everyman.'

'Feel Like A Number' 3:42
Backing Band: The Silver Bullet Band
When Seger took up the cudgels on behalf of the ordinary working man, he got angry, and nowhere more so than on this particular track. Here, the man who briefly worked on a motor assembly line in Detroit in his teens rails fiercely against being just another drone, another statistic on a sheet, another file according to the IRS. At length, he decides to cruise out of the city, head down to the sea and shout out with defiance at the ocean: 'Hey, it's me!' He's not just a number; he's a man. What gave him the idea was watching a show about computer banks and how many names were in them. As he told Steve Morse of the *Boston Globe*:

> We're all in computer banks. Lord knows how many data collections there are. Everybody is a number, and in the record industry, you're also thought of as a number – the amount you sell or whatever.

The song captures his feelings of aggression, his frustration over being an anonymous part of a workforce taken for granted by the impersonalization of modern society. There's a wall of sound, a sustained barrage of guitar, bass, drums and a Little Richard-like hammering on the keys from Robbins that weaves in and out of the verses.

'Ain't Got No Money' (Frankie Miller) 4:11

Backing band: The Muscle Shoals Rhythm Section

Frankie Miller, whose gravelly blues-rock voice made him more or less Glasgow's answer to Bob Seger, originally wrote and recorded this on his album *The Rock* in 1975. As mentioned above, 'The Fire Down Below' on *Night Moves* sounds very similar.

When subsequently asked about the matter by Steven Wheeler, Seger admitted that he was certainly listening to Miller's records when he wrote 'Fire Down Below', adding with a laugh that 'I think I paid him back by recording 'Ain't Got No Money' on the next album.' Frankie had sent him a live tape of him doing both the songs together at one of his shows in Scotland, and he had to admit that they sounded very much alike. Then again, it was pointed out, Glenn Frey's 'Smuggler's Blues' (a hit in 1985) is arguably 'Fire Down Below' in a different tempo. 'We all get affected by one another at various times', he added, but admitted he had completely overlooked the similarity until a year later when he heard the Miller tape of both songs together. That was when he decided to record the song himself, 'because I realized how much I really loved that song.'

Seger's version has Pete Carr adding some wonderful slide guitar, and Eagles' Don Felder playing the solo. Just to bring the story full circle, in 1986, The Frankie Miller Band supported Seger on some US tour dates. Whose version is the better? It's difficult to judge. Both are equally fine.

'We've Got Tonite' 4:38

Backing band: The Muscle Shoals Rhythm Section

The B-side of 'U.M.C.', 'This Old House', was later reworked with similar chords but different lyrics and melody two years later, and this was the result. What inspired Seger to do so was seeing *The Sting*, with its conversation between the characters played by Robert Redford and Dimitra Arliss, in which she says, 'I don't even know you', and he answers, 'You know me. It's two in the morning and I don't know nobody.' Seger told the *Detroit Free Press* that he wrote the song the next day, about two people who say 'I'm tired. It's late at night. I know you don't really dig me, and I don't really dig you, but this is all we've got, so let's do it'. It had been recorded during the sessions that produced *Night Moves*, but Seger held it over as he felt it wasn't 'a thematic fit' with the other tracks.

Next to *Night Moves*, this may be the loveliest song Seger ever wrote. Over-exposure and numerous cover versions, none of which can hold a candle to the original, may have tarnished it for some, but it remains a jewel in his crown. Once again, it's a masterpiece of arrangement, from the soothing piano intro, soft touches of tambourine and strings behind the first verse and chorus, the entry of drums and backing vocals on the bridge, to almost everything cutting out for a later verse and then returning in full force for an *omnes fortissimo* conclusion on the final chorus.

This was Charlotte Seger's favorite song from her son's catalogue, and after she passed away, he always retained it in his live act as a tribute to her.

The third single, it made number 13 in the US in 1978, and number 41 in the UK the following year, where in 1982 the *Nine Tonight* live version peaked at number 60. A reissue of the original recording to help promote *Greatest Hits* three years later took it to number 22.

To date, at least 50 other acts have recorded the song, the most successful being Ronan Keating & Lulu (number four, UK, 2002), Kenny Rogers & Sheena Easton (number six, US; number 28, UK, 1983) and Elkie Brooks (number 69, UK, 1987). Others include The Jeff Healey Band, Rita Coolidge & Jermaine Jackson, Shirley Bassey, Tom Jones, Conway Twitty and Barry Manilow.

Note – the 'Tonite' spelling was used only in 1978-79. Subsequent reissues on the album, single and live version were all 'Tonight'.

'Brave Strangers' 6:20

Backing Band: The Silver Bullet Band

Lyrically, this could be *Night Moves*, the sequel. Seger looks back fondly to when nights were warm, dreams were easy: 'We weren't lovers, just brave strangers, as we fought and we tumbled through the night.' For the first two minutes, there's a bustling rhythm driven by drums and piano, then it comes to a momentary but dramatic halt. Reed's sax and Doug Riley's piano usher in a slower section, as the brave strangers, 'players not arrangers', are hiding in the backwoods with the moon flying high. Another two minutes, and we return to the brisk pace at the start, while he recollects with a pang that they saw each other a few times after that, 'but we never really got it right'.

An epic cut, it was difficult to get right. Seger recalled that they tried it about 40 times in the studio, 'and some of the best takes were rather uneven but lively. I wish we had chosen one of those takes.'

'The Famous Final Scene' 5:09

Backing band: The Muscle Shoals Rhythm Section

Seger was at pains to stress that this song was not autobiographical. He aimed to write something about a lover who was saying farewell like a guest who had overstayed his welcome. It was deliberately written as a dramatic number for the stage as a contrast to the exuberance of the preponderance of rock 'n' roll tunes throughout a good concert. He explained the background in an interview with Timothy White for *Musician Player & Listener*. It was his intention, he said, to come up with something 'that would stop the show dead with its sensitivity.'

The idea came originally from 'Wasted Time', a song on the Eagles' *Hotel California*, which was about being stoned and wasted all the time; this, on the other hand, was to be about a whole relationship being wasted time. He meant to try and 'crystallize that instant in a failed relationship when two people realize, 'Hey, this is it for us. So now, how do we get out of this room?" Like many of his songs, he wrote the title first, then needed to 'back up and figure out how to get there.'

As the final track of the album, it makes an awe-inspiring finish. From a quiet opening of mainly piano and drums, it introduces some discreet lead guitar, complemented unobtrusively by strings, and later on some colorful but never overpowering organ, letting instruments come to the fore and recede again to good effect until the big finish, as the closing lines put it: 'As the light fades from the screen, from the famous final scene'.

Against The Wind (1980)

Personnel:
Bob Seger: guitar, vocals, backing vocals
The Silver Bullet Band:
Drew Abbott: guitar
Alto Reed: saxophone
Chris Campbell: bass
David Teegarden: drums, percussion
The Muscle Shoals Rhythm Section:
Barry Beckett: piano
Pete Carr, Jimmy Johnson: guitar
David Hood: bass
Roger Hawkins: drums, percussion
Randy McCormick: organ
Additional musicians:
Ginger Blake, Laura Creamer, Linda Dillard: backing vocals
Glenn Frey, Don Henley, Timothy B. Schmit: harmony vocals
Sam Clayton: percussion
Dr John: piano
Paul Harris: piano, organ
Bill Payne, Paul Harris: organ, synthesizer, piano
Doug Riley: synthesizer
Produced by Punch Andrews, Bob Seger, Muscle Shoals Rhythm Section, Bill Szymczyk
Recorded at Bayshore, Miami; Criteria, Miami; Muscle Shoals Sound Studios, Sheffield, Alabama
Release date: February 1980
Highest chart positions: UK: 26, US: 1 (six weeks)
Certification: 5x Platinum
Running time: 39:59

Bob Seger and the band followed up the release of *Stranger In Town* with a full date sheet of concerts, then took 1979 as a year off from live work in order to concentrate on the next album. During this time, he contributed backing vocals to two tracks, 'Radioactive' and 'Living In Sin', on the eponymous solo debut album by Gene Simmons of KISS, and collaborated with the Eagles, co-writing 'Heartache Tonight', which became their fifth (and last) American number one single, the first chart-topping record with which he had been involved. Most importantly, there was the matter of his next album. Everyone involved had already set the bar very high, and they were convinced the next one would be even better. The record that had a working title of *No Man's Land* appeared early in 1980, sporting the name of one of the other tracks, *Against The Wind.*

No longer 'scared of doing the softer stuff' if he really wanted, Seger was unashamed about admitting that he was aiming for a more mainstream set when they entered the studio: 'We dropped away a little bit from rockiness and went straight for the singles charts on all ten cuts, virtually.' It was more easy listening in parts than the previous two, with some of the numbers an admission of growing older and more mellow. 'Maybe it was a little too commercial,' he later conceded, 'but I wanted to make sure I had three hit singles on it.' Two reached the top ten, another the top 20 and a fourth just missed the top 40. The songs were slightly shorter than usual, with only the title track longer than five minutes, albeit edited or faded as usual for single release.

It became his first (and only) US number one LP, for six weeks during May and June. This commercial high-water mark was something he later admitted as his goal as he was 'gunning for nothing less than a chart-topping hit when (he) entered the studio.' He did it with what would be his first album since *Seven* to be completely self-composed. Later, he said that of all the records he had made to date, 'it's probably the most fulfilled I ever was as a songwriter.' Moreover, it was interesting, he added, that his band wanted to play ballads, and the Muscle Shoals musicians hankered after rock 'n' roll. Each of them had the best of both worlds.

The cover painting was commissioned by Capitol, who rang artist Jim Warren for a picture of horses. 'I don't do horses', was his response. Seger particularly wanted them, he was told. Despite his initial hesitation, he was reassured when the design won a Grammy for Best Album Package the following year.

It was also his first top 30 album in the UK, although all three singles, and a three-track EP including the title track plus two cuts from *'Live' Bullet* on the B-side later in the year, fell short of the top 75. Like Bruce Springsteen, Seger was still regarded on the other side of the Atlantic as mainly an artist for the album-buying public, whose label put out singles as a matter of course in order to promote them and perhaps find the occasional play on daytime music radio, while they still struggled to climb into the top 40.

Critical reaction was not universally favorable. In the *Los Angeles Times*, Robert Hilburn opined that it was 'close to his earlier works' but this time represented a 'mastering of the form', and he had particular praise for the reflective ballads. Others agreed it was good, if a little too 'soft' or middle of the road. Forty-five years later, Lee Zimmerman of *Classic Rock* said it 'still ranks as one of Bob's best.'

On the other hand, Dave Marsh of *Rolling Stone*, who had normally praised his work in the past, called it the worst record he had ever made, accused him of 'crafting failureproof songs that are utterly listenable and quite meaningless' and advised his readership that 'if what you need is a carefully constructed album of gravelly crooning with a half-hearted snarl thrown in once in a while for effect, you've come to the right place.' It had 'almost nothing of Seger's blustering, hard-driving concert sound ... this time the rock 'n' roll cuts are perfunctory, simply tossed in to separate the overinflated ballad 'statements'.' When shown the review, Seger shrugged it off, saying, 'I'll probably have dinner with him in six months, when he cools down.'

Nevertheless, he was at the peak of his commercial success. It coincided with the rise of what musicologists of the early 1980s would call 'heartland rock', regarded as mainly a Midwest American phenomenon. It was a loose combination of such genres as garage rock, country, soul and rock 'n' roll, with singer-songwriters extolling blue-collar themes about 'the common man', its main exponents being Seger, Bruce Springsteen, John Cougar Mellencamp and Tom Petty.

'The Horizontal Bop' 4:00

Backing band: The Silver Bullet Band

It doesn't take much guessing to work out what inspired the opening track, but there is more to it than that. Seger once again reminisces about his carefree past (another instalment of 'Night Moves'?) with more youthful memories of teenage parties, drinking, listening to music and dancing – and the other. Not a love song, so much as a lust song, basically a good-time 12-bar blues with Dr John adding a sprightly boogie on piano. After the final verse and chorus, it's all down to a one-chord jam for guitar with a solo from Seger himself, piano and sax. As the fourth, last and least successful single from the album, a double A-side with 'Her Strut', it peaked at number 42.

'You'll Accomp'ny Me' 3:58

Backing band: The Silver Bullet Band

This is something of a departure for Seger, being more of a homespun folk ballad than anything else, or as he referred to it, 'just another one of my little folk songs that I wrote in my cabin.' When he and Reed played it to the latter's girlfriend, Monica, she immediately loved it. The lyrics are delightfully simple – 'Someday lady you'll accomp'ny me', out where the rivers meet the sounding sea' – as are the melody, acoustic guitar, synth, organ and piano, with gospel-like vocals on the chorus. As the third single from the album, it made number 14. Kate and Anna McGarrigle recorded a charming French-language Cajun version, 'Tu Vas M'Accompagner', a couple of years later.

'Her Strut' 3:52

Backing band: The Silver Bullet Band

Sounding quite Stones-like, this was inspired by Seger's admiration for Jane Fonda. He wanted to write a song about how women had 'become so confident and stepped out so much', and he saw her as a great role model. That's a brave statement to make, and any man writing a song with those intentions runs the risk of being accused of sexism, or perhaps even worse, being called patronizing. Somehow it comes across as a little naïve in its sentiments, singing the praises of a woman 'totally committed to major independence, but she's a lady through and through – she'll bruise some, she'll hurt some too, but oh, they love to watch her strut'.

Some reviewers thought it was demeaning to women, suggesting it was ill-advised or maybe trying to cock a snook at political correctness and failing badly. Music journalists Jimmy Guterman and Owen O'Donnell called it a 'bewildering, lame ditty', and branded Seger for sounding 'like an aging high school football jerk who never grew out of thinking of 'girls' as either virgins or whores', while Dave Marsh accused him of 'belittling women when they try to assert themselves.' He defended himself against accusations of misogyny, saying that he loved the very title of the song as conjuring up an image, and 'that at the bottom line, it's human nature, that men are *still* gonna love women for being sexual in spite of all this other stuff.'

Whatever one may think of the lyrics, it's a good vehicle for Drew Abbott's best snarling guitar solos, although it tends to be one of those songs that starts off in mid-gear and fails to rise any higher.

'No Man's Land' 3:41

Backing band: The Muscle Shoals Rhythm Section

One of Seger's most reflective lyrics, this is a mid-paced folk number with acoustic guitar, piano and prominent organ. No man's land is a middle ground, a safe place to be 'between the ever restless crowds and the silence of your room'. He sings it in a relaxed, reassuring style, and it ends with a superb soaring solo from Pete Carr, which fades perhaps a little too soon.

'Long Twin Silver Line' 4:15

Backing band: The Muscle Shoals Rhythm Section

By this time, it's clear that he is tending to pace the out-and-out rockers with more gentle fare. This is rock 'n' roll all the way, a song that takes the train, 'rolling on down the track', as a metaphor for life being a never-ending journey. The lyrics describe a trip across America, but could just as easily be taken as life itself being a never-ending exploration, with a relentless powerhouse of guitar and piano right up to the fadeout.

'Against The Wind' 5:32

Backing band: The Silver Bullet Band

Love, life, perseverance and even ageing are the themes of the title track, and in the process, it became undoubtedly one of his classic songs of reflection. The first verse refers to his relationship with Janey Dinsdale, 'and the mountains that we moved', how he was sure it would never end. Another line runs, 'I wish I didn't know now what I didn't know then'. When he told management and band that he wasn't sure about that because it sounded 'grammatically funny', they all reassured him: 'that's a great line', if not the best in the whole song. To his surprise, he saw the same line on a few other songs soon afterwards, in one by Poison and one in a country song. It was distinctive, but a sad one when read or listened to in context. The years roll by, and the voice in the song finds himself 'surrounded by strangers' he thought were his friends. Later still, he finds the drifter's days are behind him, and life is all deadlines and commitments; he's older now but still running against the wind.

Seger told Mike Ragogna of *HuffPost* that it was a song about how 'you've got to be brave when you're running against the wind, and you've got to have conviction to make it through, and I think that's true. You can't lose your confidence, and you just have to keep going, and know that you've got something worthwhile.' It's also 'about trying to move ahead, keeping your sanity and integrity at the same time. The people in that song have weathered the storm, and it's made them much better.'

In keeping with the somber tone of the lyrics, the accompaniment is suitably tender and sympathetic, with acoustic guitar, bass and drums very much in the background. Glenn Frey sings backing vocals, and Paul Harris's work throughout on piano, with subtle touches of organ, really sets the seal on what is by any standards a masterpiece.

Extracted as a single, it reached number five in the US. Much covered, the most high profile versions were by Garth Brooks, an easy listening jazz rendition by Paul Anka, and most memorably of all, by The Highwaymen country supergroup – Waylon Jennings, Willie Nelson, Johnny Cash and one of Seger's original songwriting heroes, Kris Kristofferson.

'Good For Me' 4:01

Backing band: The Muscle Shoals Rhythm Section

The album's main love song is a simple waltz-tempo tune; it is rather like a chant over and over that never deviates from the basic chord sequence. Maybe a bridge somewhere would have made all the difference, but to compensate for the lack of one, it is arranged well with ample contrast between the verses, mainly acoustic guitar and piano-led, and the choruses, where drums and backing vocals build it up and give it something of a gospel feeling.

'Betty Lou's Gettin' Out Tonight' 2:53

Backing band: The Silver Bullet Band

'Brace yourself now, take a deep breath', goes one line from the first verse. Unlike the two earlier rock 'n' roll songs on the album, there's no innuendo and no dubious breaches of PC about the lyrics in this one. Seger sings his heart out, while piano, guitar and sax are all steaming in unison almost from the word go, and especially on the solos. The legacy of Chuck Berry and Larry Williams is safe in their hands, and Seger rarely recorded anything more infectious than this.

'Fire Lake' 3:32

Backing band: The Muscle Shoals Rhythm Section

This was several years in the making, having originally been intended for *Beautiful Loser* but not completed in time. When asked to explain the subject matter, Seger said it was about taking a risk and stepping out of personal expectations, or one's own comfort zone. More specifically, it was 'about risking love, chucking it all and just heading off with a bunch of wild people.' It would always be one of his favorite lyrics, as he liked the metaphor of living on the edge, 'you never see a lake burning'. He had wanted this to be the first single released off the album, and never thought Capitol would agree to it. Andrews persuaded them to change their minds; it was issued as a 45 in January, and they were rewarded with a number six hit.

Most of the song is based around a recurring pattern of the chords G, D and Em, the verses accompanied by a medium tempo of piano and acoustic guitar, interrupted by a short bridge of one major and three minors before the drums join in a little more heavily and the rest of the song returns to the opening pattern until fading. Three Eagles – Glenn Frey, Don Henley and Timothy B. Schmit – contribute backing vocals. Some diehard fans were amazed, not to say disappointed, when they heard this as a taster from the album. He admitted that perhaps the edge had gone, and the record was pretty mellow. The Eagles' influence was inevitable as he was hanging out a lot with them at the time.

'Shinin' Brightly' 4:25

Backing band: The Muscle Shoals Rhythm Section

To conclude comes a song with echoes of 'Till It Shines' from the previous album. As with 'Good For Me', the melody and chord sequence are very simple, with folksy acoustic guitar and piano prominent throughout, while Reed from The Silver Bullet Band adds some excellent sax embellishments as usual. The message is equally straightforward, one of hope and optimism that the dark clouds are rolling away, the rough times are past and it's all 'startin' to feel good again'. Towards the end, there's a little call-and-response routine involving Seger and the backing singers.

The Distance (1982)

Personnel:
Bob Seger: vocals, harmony vocals, guitar
The Silver Bullet Band:
Chris Campbell: bass
Craig Frost: organ, piano
Alto Reed: saxophone
Muscle Shoals Rhythm Section:
Barry Beckett: piano, organ
Pete Carr: guitar
David Hood: bass
Roger Hawkins: drums
Randy McCormick: electric piano
Additional musicians:
Drew Abbott, Don Felder, Davey Johnstone, Danny Kortchmar, Waddy Wachtel: guitar
Roy Bittan: piano
Michael Boddicker: synthesizer
Bobbye Hall: percussion
Russ Kunkel: drums
Bill Payne: piano, synthesizer
Additional vocals:
Ginger Blake, Laura Creamer, Linda Dillard, Shaun Murphy, Joan Sliwin
Bonnie Raitt, Glenn Frey: harmony vocals
Produced by Jimmy Iovine
Recorded: Studio 55, LA; Crystal Sound Recording, LA; Muscle Shoals Sound Studios, Sheffield, Alabama
Release date: 13 December 1982
Highest chart positions: UK: 45, US: 5
Certification: 2x Platinum
Running time: 41:05

There were no concerts in 1981 and 1982, while Seger, the band and others completed the next studio album. He had decided on a few changes this time. Instead of co-producing with Andrews, he chose Jimmy Iovine, best known for his recent work with Bruce Springsteen and Tom Petty & The Heartbreakers, and a sadly underrated last album by The Motors. His first choice had been Bill Szymczyk, who had helmed the last few albums by the now disbanded Eagles, and assisted him and Andrews on *Against The Wind*, but Szymczyk was in the throes of a divorce at the time. Iovine turned out to be quite a demanding producer, and for Seger, it was the first time that he had worked with one who didn't merely tell him what not to write, but encouraged him to keep on writing because what he already had wasn't quite good enough. This process lasted for about ten months, and then another four months putting it together.

He also wanted to select more musicians from outside the close groupings of The Silver Bullet Band and The Muscle Shoals Rhythm Section. With the latter, recording took far less time than the former. As an experiment, he had decided to take the nucleus from The Bullets, namely Chris Campbell on bass, Craig Frost on keyboards and Alto Reed on sax, and bring in different players as needed. Guitarist Drew Abbott and drummer Dave Teegarden, who had worked with him for some time, were annoyed with this new arrangement and left – or were simply released – to be replaced by Dawayne Bailey and former Grand Funk Railroad drummer Don Brewer.

After watching the Woody Allen movie *Annie Hall*, Seger had the idea of an album about relationships. At length, he decided that it would risk sounding too 'maudlin'. Meanwhile, Iovine 'got more and more demanding', so he thought he would focus less on the relationship theme.

As usual, there would be too many songs to fit on one album. Initially, with so much material to choose from, he considered making it a double, something in which Bruce Springsteen, fresh from his success with *The River*, was happy to encourage. He changed his mind on the grounds that times were hard and that such a release would be too expensive for many of his fans, especially as records already cost too much, and 'the bottom line was the economy.' As someone who had always stayed firmly grounded in Detroit, he knew the recession had hit the local auto industry hard. Moreover, he also firmly believed that he'd never heard a great double studio album, beyond The Beatles' *White Album,* that wouldn't have been greatly improved by being reduced to a single long player.

By the time it was released in the US in December 1982, the eight-track cartridge format for albums was becoming a thing of the past. Seger asked Capitol to issue the record on that format as well as cassette, as he still had a considerable fan base for whom old habits died hard, and many of them preferred buying their music on cartridges for in-car listening.

If *Against The Wind,* for all its chart-topping success, didn't quite match everyone's expectations, its successor certainly did. *Los Angeles Times* reviewer Dennis Hunt noted that it was 'loaded with robust rock 'n' roll', and nearly the equal of *Stranger In Town*. Another *Rolling Stone* writer, David Fricke, called it not a very happy album, but a triumphant one. One further measure of the quality of *The Distance*, in retrospect sometimes considered one of Seger's finest albums ever, was the effect it had on the journalist who was probably his most famous critic. Having praised him in earlier times and then given his previous album, ironically his most successful to date, a real roasting, Richard Marsh could hardly be more fulsome in his praise this time. (Tell us, Bob, did you have the lunch you planned with him after his last diatribe?)

> Most superstars are indeed immobilized by their success (that is, both the overt and covert theme of *Against The Wind*). But the great ones find a way

to struggle through and speak the truth again. And that is why *The Distance* is a record that moves me to the core and makes me want to apologize to Bob Seger. Consider it tendered.

'Even Now' 4:31

Backing band: The Silver Bullet Band

Seger said that this and 'Shame On The Moon' were the best tracks on the album, even 'flawless'. Springsteen, Stevie Nicks and Tom Petty all said that 'Even Now' had to be the first single, as it was in the UK, where it reached a disappointing number 73, and the second in the US, making it to number 12. The lyrics tell of his dedication to his partner Janey Dinsdale, with whom he had a relationship for 11 years and with whom he had come close to splitting about a year before it was recorded, and he 'sat around devastated.' Ironically, not long after the album was released, they did break up for good.

As a pop-rock single and as a production, this record is well-nigh flawless. The magnificently bombastic chord sequence on the intro forms an immediate hook for the listener, while the prominent use of Hammond organ and piano throughout much of the song – the latter with its echoes of the flourishes of keys on ABBA's 'Dancing Queen' and the song that confessed to unashamedly stealing its hooks, Elvis Costello & The Attractions' 'Oliver's Army' – make an astonishingly infectious sound. The whole song, arrangement and above production add up to what resulted in one of his very best singles ever, certainly as regards the more up-tempo fare – very different from the haunting 'Night Moves', but in its own way an almost equally potent experience. In its adrenaline burst of thunderous energy, it may have an echo of 'Hollywood Nights', but it's certainly not a lame retread, more a worthy cousin.

Even the big finish is quite spectacular. After Seger's vocal finishes on the last title phrase, he's followed by a single organ chord sustained for about 20 seconds, aided and abetted by little but still masterful flourishes on lead guitar, piano and drums. He certainly knew what he was doing when he hired Iovine as producer.

'Makin' Thunderbirds' 2:58

Backing band: The Silver Bullet Band

This is the first of two consecutive tracks that Seger said were 'sort of a two-part novel on the state of the Midwest as I see it.' Reviewers were quick to draw comparisons between these numbers and similarly themed songs on contemporary releases by Bruce Springsteen and Billy Joel, labelling them 'recession rock'. This song is, on the surface, a pounding, fully-charged 12-bar blues (in the style of Dylan's 'Highway 61 Revisited', to name one of several), with a wall of heavy guitar chords, pounding beat, harmony vocals from Bonnie Raitt, plus a break with boogie piano and sax that will have anybody on their feet and dancing. Then you listen to the words and realize that this wasn't written as a party song. It's a reference to the struggling motor industry, looking back on how good business was a few years before, when 'we were young and proud'. It didn't last, though: 'Now the years have flown and the plants are changed, and you're lucky if you work', he warns us. It proves that behind a lot of good-time songs lurks a note of sobering realism. Seger was writing from experience, having spent three months in his youth at Ford fitting rubber mouldings around the windscreens before leaving as it hurt his hands too much (no job for a dedicated musician), and he wanted to contribute a song about the experience. It was originally written as a slow blues, but he changed it as Andrews was no fan of the genre.

'Boomtown Blues' 3:38
Backing band: The Silver Bullet Band
Part two of the novel was said to have been written about the 'boomtown' Houston, a hive of activity, a prosperous area where everybody seemed to be leading a comfortable life. Everyone was under pressure to work hard in order to generate wealth, making the perception that they were trapped in a comfortable paradise, or as one verse ends, 'stuck here in heaven with those boomtown blues'. A monotonous life where everyone's working to live, where material gain seems more important than anything else, leads to discontent and emptiness. Meanwhile, other people are envious; 'They'd love to be in your shoes, how come you've got those boomtown blues?' There's a hard-hitting, insistent rhythm from guitar and drums, almost like slowed-down funk, that steps up a gear, or two, with the sax break early on that returns towards the fadeout.

'Shame On The Moon' (Rodney Crowell) 4:55
The only non-original on the album, this was written by country singer Rodney Crowell, who was at the time married to Johnny Cash's daughter, Rosanne, herself quite a star in country music. Don Henley had originally advised Seger to listen to Rodney's album, and he was so thrilled with it that he immediately took it over to Alto's house to play it to him. The sax player's girlfriend was immediately struck by this song, and Seger said, 'We cut it in six hours and got a miracle track.' Glenn Frey added harmony vocals.

It's a gentle number about how misunderstandings and lack of perception in human relationships can end in heartbreak. As an easy-on-the-ear country tune that would have fitted neatly onto *Against The Wind*, with acoustic guitar and gentle piano backed up by a relaxed drum shuffle, it became not only a major country hit but also Bob's sixth top ten and biggest US single to date, spending four weeks at number two, although it failed to chart in the UK.

'Love's The Last To Know' 4:26
Seger really bares his soul on this ballad, which, in its simplicity, as it portrays the aftermath of a relationship that has gone badly wrong, sounds like a return to the unvarnished, intimate songs on *Brand New Morning* over a

decade earlier. There is more of a full complement of musicians here, but his vocal stands alone without any harmonies, while the main instruments are piano, holding everything together, and drums, which are alternately quite forceful in some places, especially on the piano-led break, and suitably restrained in others. Organ adds a little color, as does a small amount of guitar from regular Elton John sideman Davey Johnstone.

'Roll Me Away' 4:39
Backing band: The Silver Bullet Band
For years, Seger had wanted to take a motorcycle trip to Jackson Hole, Wyoming, and it was everything he had hoped it would be. The day he set out, it was a blazing hot summer, he recalled; all he had on were his shorts, and he had to put his feet up on the handlebars to keep them from boiling on the engine. 'It was just silence and feeling nature.' Sometimes called one of the greatest evocations of man, motorcycle and the freedom of the highway ever committed to vinyl, this song celebrates that journey, an epic song recalling the freedom of rolling across the high plains, deep into the mountains, then watching a young hawk flying and feeling his soul begin to rise. He always delivers his vocals with passion, and here producer and musicians help create a genuine atmosphere for those words.

The first 40 seconds suggest that maybe it's going to be a ballad, with subdued piano, organ, bass and drums behind the vocal – then the drums really kick in with power. In particular, Roy Bittan's sweeping piano work, Craig Frost's organ and Michael Boddicker's synth all combine to make this a grand musical statement, the sound that Bruce Springsteen and Meat Loaf (plus the teams behind them) had all discovered to make such powerful records over the previous few years. The album's third single, it peaked at number 28 in the US, though it was another that failed to make the charts in the UK.

'House Behind A House' 4:00
Backing band: The Silver Bullet Band
Isolation, concealment of feelings and trying to avoid facing the inevitable are the key themes in this lyric. Two people have reached the end of the road, and at what point do they finally admit it? The sadness of lonely faces staring at their hands while the walls keep closing in is a stark one. Musically, it's not the most adventurous song, most of it clinging to two chords (and a third briefly about halfway through), while for the last minute or so the sax is jamming away on one chord, with occasional repetition of the title being sung again, until it fades.

'Comin' Home' 6:06
Backing band: Muscle Shoals Rhythm Section
Equally poignant is this gentle song about a man who's just spent ten years in the city lights to his hometown with its sleepless nights, and dreams that

went wrong. Tired of being alone, he returns home and finds the place has hardly changed, but he doesn't want to admit to his failure.

The longest track on the album, it's divided into two; the song takes up the first three and a half minutes, with Seger's vocals backed mainly by piano and acoustic guitar, to be followed by a passage consisting of two chords with synth, sax and backing vocals, and again fading without anything else happening. It's an attractive number as far as it goes, but one feels that a little more variation in the structure would have held more attention.

'Little Victories' 5:52

Backing band: The Silver Bullet Band

Following two songs that don't quite deliver, the album ends on an upswing with one that does. Another relationship has failed, and in the writer's words, it's basically about not letting it pull you down, but rather resolving 'to pull yourself out of a hole when something crushing happens to you.' When night falls and there's nobody around, it's a cruel time – so 'take a lesson from the trees, watch the way they learn to bend with each breeze'. Every little victory counts. After three minutes, there's almost a false ending before the song takes flight again. Seger and Waddy Wachtel share guitar duties on this one, with some smoldering solos to produce plenty of light and shade between them.

Non-Album Single

'Understanding' 3:42 b/w **'East L.A.'** 5:14

Released in October 1984

Produced by Bob Seger and Punch Andrews

Probably one of the relationship-themed songs recorded for possible inclusion on *The Distance*, this is a mid-tempo song about finding fulfilment in love and the union of two like-minded souls. Based largely around piano, organ and powerful drumming, plus good use of gospel-tinged backing vocals, it's not that far removed from some of Elton John's best of the period. One of ten songs on the original motion picture soundtrack of *Teachers*, a black comedy-drama starring Nick Nolte and JoBeth Williams, it was one of three to be released as singles (the others being by 38 Special and Joe Cocker), with 'Understanding' reaching number 17 in the US, the only one to reach the top 20. In *Cash Box*, the reviewer called it...

> ...by and large successful in bringing together a good, singable melody, meaningful lyrics and superb performances. Despite a chorus that remains on one plateau and never fully takes hold, the song clearly captures the power inherent in its words, which deal with the personal quest for growth and knowledge, and allows Seger's rich, honest and touching vocals to shine through.

The B-side, not on the soundtrack album, is probably another *The Distance* outtake, a relaxed atmospheric number with an almost hypnotic piano and drum riff, about the joys of sitting with his lady on a warm night, 'drinkin' warm beer in the soft summer air' (itself almost an exact lift from Springsteen's 'Jungleland'), and looking across the city and those starlit hills.

Like A Rock (1986)

Personnel:
Bob Seger: vocals, guitar, piano
The Silver Bullet Band:
Chris Campbell: bass
Craig Frost: organ, piano, synthesizer
Alto Reed: baritone and tenor saxophone, tenor saxophone, organ
Additional musicians:
Dawayne Bailey: acoustic and electric guitar
Pete Carr, Dann Huff: guitar
Mark Chatfield: electric guitar
Bill Payne: piano, synthesizer
David Cole: synthesizer
Don Brewer, Russ Kunkel, Gary Mallaber, John Robinson: drums
Paulinho da Costa: percussion
Gary Grant, Jerry Hey: trumpet
Gary Herbig, Kim Hutchcroft, Marc Russo, Ernie Watts: saxophone
Bill Reichenbach Jr.: trombone
Fred Tackett: acoustic guitar
Rick Vito: slide and acoustic guitar
Laura Creamer, Mark Creamer, Donny Gerrard, Don Henley, Douglas Kibble, Shaun Murphy, Timothy B. Schmit, The Weather Girls (Izora Armstead, Martha Wash): backing vocals
Produced by Punch Andrews, David N. Cole, Bob Seger
Release date: 27 March 1986
Highest chart positions: UK: 35, US: 3
Certification: Platinum
Running time: 40:28 (standard); 43.48 (plus 1986 bonus track); 50.11 (plus later bonus tracks)

Like A Rock was some three years in the making. At first, Seger had decided he wanted to produce it entirely himself, and that meant months of learning how everything worked in the studio. 'It was an experiment,' he said, 'and the whole thing got out of hand. There was nobody to say 'no' to me and I ended up recording 25 songs in four different cities.' The result was meant to have been two different albums, with the first released in 1984, until he changed his mind and scrapped all but two songs, namely 'American Storm' and 'Like A Rock'. Once the album was ready, he planned to name it *American Storm*, but after Springsteen and Jackson Browne had released politically-charged albums, namely *Born In The U.S.A.* and *Lives In The Balance*, he changed his mind and used the other song title instead.

By this time, he had settled into a routine of calling on outside musicians when appropriate to supplement the three remaining Silver Bullet musicians. It's notable that this was the only Seger studio album on which he and his band appeared on the front of the sleeve. The Muscle Shoals Rhythm Section were now history as far as he was concerned.

The man who had recently been through two relationships that had run their course, and who was happy with loving and creating rock music into middle age with some of the finest players possible, was proud to be making records for people of his age group. It was a matter of growing up, he said in an interview with *Creem* to mark the release of the album.

> From the time I was 20 until I was 30, I didn't sell a whole lot of records, but I was doing a lot of rock 'n' roll. That's the way I felt at the time. Maybe during the period when I was 30 to 40, I was getting more mature, writing about older themes. I'm sure 'Like A Rock' doesn't mean much to someone who's 20, but I gotta write what I know about.

The album was not quite as successful as its predecessors, and Seger admitted that he wasn't completely happy with it. He later said that 'Tightrope' was fun, but he didn't capture it the way he wanted to, and he didn't really like the synthesizer songs. He hated 'The Aftermath' and thought 'Sometimes' was pretty average.

'American Storm' 4:17

As is so often the case, track one is a real tour de force. Carr's guitar chords, Payne's rippling piano and Kunkel's powerful drums blast straight in on a hard-rocking number with Seger absolutely singing his heart out. As Chris Willman of the *Los Angeles Times* commented, it was 'an anti-drug anthem so artfully done you'd never guess it was an anti-drug anthem.' It's one of those songs that is catchy enough to lodge itself in the listener's brain after a few hearings, and at the same time makes an impact with the sheer conviction that the singer and musicians are clearly putting into it.

Seger wrote it after reading *Wired*, a biography of John Belushi, comedian, actor and recent drug casualty. Having seen his alcoholic father walk out on the family when he was only a boy, he knew all about the perils of addiction. For a while, he believed and hoped that cocaine and other substance abuse were a trend that would die out, but it shocked him that the problem was now apparently escalating. The song, he said unequivocally, was about people ruining their lives by doing drugs. 'You never feel the heat from police', he told *The New York Times*. 'You never feel warm. Drugs are a wall of sin. Drugs are taking over like an American storm.' To him, the key line in the song was 'You never feel the need'. 'You never feel anything when you're on drugs. You're numb. You're afraid to feel for one reason or another, and that's why you turn to drugs. I want to see people not do that.'

A Chicago radio station, WLUP-FM, spliced it together with 'Even Now', calling them 'the same song' and saying that the new one was 'ridiculously derivative' of the others. Seger conceded that they were the same tempo, and admitted that one could say that it was also like 'Hollywood Nights' 'because there's a certain tempo for rock 'n' roll.' After all, there were only so many chords and so many tempos, 'but you just try to say things a little better.'

The album's first single, it reached number 17 in the US and number 78 in the UK.

'Like A Rock' 5:56

The title track and the album's longest, Seger told the *New York Times*:

> It was inspired partly by the end of a relationship that had lasted for 11 years. You wonder where all that time went. But beyond that, it expresses my feeling that the best years of your life are in your late teens, when you have no special commitments and no career. It's your last blast of fun before heading into the cruel world.

The first three verses look back to when he was 18 years old, feeling like number one, working for peanuts and not having a care in the world, still believing in his dreams. Time moves on, and the last two find him 20 years in the future, late at night by the light of a ghostly moon, wondering where his youth had gone. To *Cash Box*, it was an 'emotional ballad of perseverance and commitment', while *Billboard* called it a 'slow-paced, rough-edged ballad [that] mourns the certainties of youth.' From the quietest of openings with his voice accompanied only by guitars, Dawayne Bailey's acoustic and Rick Vito's delicate electric, it builds gently throughout as bass, drums and organ come in at the right time and then step back. Vito's solos on slide guitar later in the song and the discreet backing vocals all lend color to the haunting atmosphere of a bittersweet contemplation from the standpoint of middle age. As the album's second single, the song peaked in the US at number 12.

For some years, Seger had actively resisted the mere idea of allowing his music to be licensed for TV commercials and turned down requests from General Motors, Coors Beers and others. He only had a change of heart when he was in a restaurant one day, and a worker walked in, recognized him and asked him why he didn't do something in that line for the car companies. As he and his father before him had worked in the industry, he felt that it seemed right, and so he called the advertising executives. Within a few years, 'Like A Rock' had become synonymous with Chevrolet pickup truck advertisements. Nevertheless, he insisted that this would be his first and last commercial, and it was very unlikely that he'd ever do another.

'Miami' 4:40

A brighter, quite optimistic song in tone, or in the words of *Cash Box*, 'a more relaxed, melodic outing', *Miami* is a song about the Mariel Boatlift in 1980, when over 125,000 Cuban refugees fled Havana over a six-month period, seeking a better life in Florida. Taken at mid-tempo, this time Reed's playing is bolstered by four more sax players, plus additional brass with two more musicians on trumpet and one on trombone. There's a backdrop of synthesizer throughout most of the song, plus backing vocals from two Eagles, Henley and Schmit this time, and the result is a sound of celebration. As a piece of music, it was more or less tailor-made for TV and was appropriately featured in one episode of *Miami Vice*, a crime drama TV series that ran for five years in the 1980s. The fourth and least successful single from the album, it reached number 70 in the US. It was, however, one of the numbers that Seger admitted he really loved.

'The Ring' 5:35

The song that Seger called his personal favorite on the album is a stark tale about a couple's marriage from their teens to middle age after the children have left home. Although the marriage starts well, the husband seems complacent while his wife was the one who had sacrificed her earliest hopes of going to college and making a career for herself. Now the children have gone, and every day the husband comes home, they talk over supper and he's the first to turn in – 'another day just ends'. Then the song ends with the line 'She never looks at the ring'.

It's hardly an uncommon scenario, but in a few sharp verses, he conveys the sad story so effectively. He expressed disappointment that it was never played on the radio – perhaps all the stations found it too harrowing – but was thrilled that Don Henley, always an honest judge, really liked it. For a song with such a sad message, it's appropriate that the whole musical mood is restrained, the sonic equivalent of a modern photograph in monochrome. All the guitars are acoustic (and this is the only track on which Seger plays the instrument here), with no dazzling solo from Rick Vito or anyone else, with piano, organ and synthesizer sounding like strings.

'Tightrope' (Craig Frost, Seger) 4:31

This was the first of two songs for which Craig Frost wrote the music and Seger supplied lyrics afterwards, the latter admitting that both numbers 'represent the dark days.' He was at a low ebb when he wrote them, feeling lonesome and shell-shocked at the end of an 11-year relationship. There's something of a thread connecting these and also one song on each of the two previous albums, namely 'Against The Wind' and then 'Even Now', the latter ironically having been composed after he and Janey Dinsdale had come close to breaking up. On this album, they have reached the end of the road. Now he's welcoming her 'to the tightrope between memory and pain'. Some of the lyrics are quite angry, with equally impassioned vocals to match; others are more resigned.

There's also a clear musical difference between this and much of the preceding tracks. No gently-strummed acoustic guitars, no soothing piano or organ, but some quite fierce, growling guitar work from Vito and a semi-discordant, even jagged riff on synthesizers that suggests an unexpected about-turn onto the outer shores of both synth rock and progressive rock.

'The Aftermath' (Frost, Seger) 3:30

The story continues, but whereas 'Tightrope' was musically more restrained, 'The Aftermath' rocks out with more passion. This time, she's dressed up to the nines, the champagne is on ice and she's evidently out for a good time. She's taken a few falls, is bouncing back and living through the aftermath. Seger is rocking out much harder and perhaps accepting the parting of the ways with resignation. As he commented, though not referring to it in the lyrics, the relationship in real life wasn't meant to be, and they were better off apart. As his old friend Glenn Frey told him, 'your career is a harsh mistress'. There's a tougher, more insistent beat to this song than the previous one, more heavy on the drums and synthesizer.

'Sometimes' 3:31

After three somewhat darker songs, the next two come as light relief. It's another one about relationships and communication problems, though nothing too lyrically profound. 'Sometimes I move in chains but never feel the pain' are the opening lines; later, it's a case of 'I want to leave behind this hopeless maze of broken dreams and endless days'. Everything is set to an upbeat pop-rock number, featuring a powerful break about halfway through with horns, boogie piano and a guitar solo. Although not quite in the same class as 'American Storm', it's an infectious, powerful tune that might have been worth considering as a single.

'It's You' 4:03

This is the optimistic song of a man who had recently fallen on hard times and has now found the love of his life: 'searchin' for a light to see me through, I look up and I just can't help smilin', it's you'. It's pleasant, and to quote *Cash Box*, it 'has a mellow country inflection with the customary Seger rock edge', to say nothing of a catchy hook on synthesizer. Although the preceding song might have made a better single, this one was chosen as the second 45 from the album and reached number 52 in the US.

'Somewhere Tonight' 4:25

The final track, for those who only bought the vinyl, is a return to the ballads. The themes are loneliness, a passion that's beginning to fade and emotional isolation. The lyrics begin, 'someone's reaching out to someone who's refusing, someone's walking out the door'. The atmosphere of sadness, even doom, is reinforced by the imagery of winter winds that come howling, and a cold wind blowing in from the north. It brings to mind the line that Seger apparently contributed to the chart-topping Eagles tune – 'There's gonna be a heartache tonight'. It's all set to a soft backing of piano and a synth sounding like strings. It's poignant and again enjoyable enough, although not one of his best slower tunes.

'Fortunate Son' (John Fogerty) 3:20

Those who purchased the CD version at the time, or the 'American Storm' single and played the B-side, had an additional track, Seger's version of 'Fortunate Son', recorded live in concert at Cobo Hall on 31 March 1983. The general opinion is that, good as the original by Creedence Clearwater Revival (a double-A side top three hit in December 1969) may be, this is even superior. For the most part, they follow the arrangement of the original, although their version is almost a minute longer with an extension of the outro, repeating the three-chord sequence and the refrain a few more times. Reed is credited on organ this time, although it's difficult to make out in the sheer wall of sound.

Fogerty had always been supportive of the soldiers who were sent to fight in Vietnam. He wrote the song as he had been incensed by the fact that eligible young men with enough money, or else connections with those in high places, could easily avoid being drafted. Some regard it as one of his best songs ever. As the writer and performer of an anti-war anthem himself in his younger days, '2 + 2 = ?', Seger was well-placed to cover a song on the theme, and spits out lines like 'I ain't no senator's son' with equal venom.

Deluxe Edition Bonus Tracks

'Shakedown' (Seger, Harold Faltermeyer, Keith Forsey) 4:03

Produced by Harold Faltermeyer and Keith Forsey

In 1984, Glenn Frey had a number two hit in the US with 'The Heat Is On', written by Faltermeyer and Forsey, from the soundtrack of the Eddie Murphy action-comedy *Beverly Hills Cop*. Two or three years later, he was invited to record the theme for *Beverly Hills Cop II*, but had laryngitis at the time. According to another version, he declined as he disliked the backing track and didn't want to be involved. Irving Azoff, who was the Eagles' manager (and who kept closely in touch with them all, though they were then on their '14-year vacation' and not on the best of terms with each other), asked Seger, a longtime friend, if he could do it. The backing track had already been recorded with Faltermeyer on Synclavier, Forsey on percussion and Dann Huff on guitar. All it needed was lyrics (which on the demo consisted of 'blah blah blah, shakedown, breakdown'), and somebody to write and sing them. They had about ten days to complete the job. Seger was sent the track, wrote the lyrics in about three days, sang it one night, and Timothy B. Schmit of the Eagles joined him in the studio to finish the recording. Faltermeyer and Forsey did all the rest.

In the summer of 1987, he said, 'Lordy-be, it went to number one.' It was his 31st hit, and came 18 years after his first. For him, it was a song that just dropped into his lap, a 'kind of an oddity in [his] career, it was a fluke.' It was his sole chart-topping 45 in the US and Canada, though it only managed number 88 in the UK. (The 7" and 12" versions are both the same, with no extended remix of the latter released.)

Lordy-be, indeed. The man who had sung a few years earlier, 'Don't try to take me to a disco', had finally claimed a number one single with – well, a disco record? It was regarded by some as a typical 1980s conveyor belt production line piece of synth-dance-pop, his unmistakable vocals for many being its saving grace. Some loved it, but others thought that judging his contribution to American rock music by his only number one was rather akin to doing the same for Chuck Berry *vis-à-vis* his 1972 *double entendre* singalong, the thoroughly irritating 'My Ding-A-Ling', his biggest hit ever on both sides of the Atlantic. However, Frey congratulated his old friend, saying, 'At least we kept the money in Michigan!'

In 1988, the song was nominated for both the Academy Award for Best Original Song and the Golden Globe Award for Best Original Song, and also performed at the 60th Academy Awards, Los Angeles, in 1988 by Little Richard.

'Blue Monday' (Dave Bartholomew) 2:23

Produced by Bob Seger

This old R&B classic, as made popular in the mid-1950s by Smiley Lewis and then Fats Domino, was one of several oldies Seger and the band recorded in 1988 as a warm-up for early sessions that would result in *The Fire Inside*, his next solo album. It would appear on the 1989 film *Road House*, starring Patrick Swayze, with a soundtrack on Arista also featuring music by The Jeff Healey Band, Little Feat and Otis Redding. Featuring Steve Lukather (guitar), Bob Glaub (bass), Roy Bittan and Jai Winding (keyboards), and Russ Kunkel (drums), between them they pull off a well-nigh faultless recreation of the original without adding anything new.

Standalone Cuts

In July 1986, Seger and The Silver Bullet Band began a 106-date tour of North America, finishing in March 1987 with seven dates at the Joe Louis Arena in Detroit, selling an estimated one and a half million tickets in the process. By then, he was ready for what he called the pace of a more 'normal' life. After a 12-year span in which he released eight very successful albums, two of them live double sets, and played about 600 concerts in North America and Europe, he could afford to slow down. Like many other artists of his generation, he no longer felt tied to what had been the conventional pattern for a successful artist to release a new album every two or three years.

There was also much going on in his personal life. In 1987, he married actress Annette Sinclair, a union that ended in divorce a year later with no children. At that time, he moved to Los Angeles as he thought it would be really good for his writing to live there, surrounded by the entertainment community, but then realized it turned out to be the exact opposite, more like 24 hours a day of entertainment. His mother fell ill around the same time and was hospitalized for a long period. Much time was spent visiting her and keeping her company until she passed away in February 1989.

In terms of songs completed and recorded but never released, his industry was remarkable. He admitted that he wrote 'too much', and had no shortage of spare items for films. It's only fair to assume that the best material went on his albums, while the movies had to make do with what might have been regarded as filler.

'Living Inside My Heart' 3:28
Produced by Bob Seger and Punch Andrews
Probably an outtake from the *Like A Rock* sessions, this was the love theme from the original motion picture soundtrack of *About Last Night* (EMI America, 1986), a rom-com starring Rob Lowe and Demi Moore. It's another of those warm, gentle, easy-on-the-ear ballads that were second nature to him around this time, celebrating a perfect relationship with someone who 'gets me through the hard times'. Piano, acoustic guitar, synthesizer and drums provide the accompaniment, and once again it's pleasant and difficult to fault, if not exceptional. Other artists on the album included John Waite, Jermaine Jackson and Sheena Easton.

'The Little Drummer Boy' (Harry Simeone, Henry Onorati, Katherine Kennicott Davis) 3:27
Produced by Jimmy Iovine
One of 15 tracks on a various artists album, *A Very Special Christmas* (A&M Records, 1987), in aid of the Special Olympics fund, the song was originally written around 1941 and is said to have been loosely based on an old Czech carol. The lyrics tell of a poor boy who was summoned by the Magi to visit Jesus in his cradle, and as he had no present to bring with him, he played

on his drum instead. Seger's vocals contrast effectively with the choral-style backing vocals from Laura Creamer, Rosemary Butler and others. Nils Lofgren on guitar joins Seger's regular musicians, including Craig Frost, Alto Reed, Rick Vito and Don Brewer, with Jimmy Iovine producing. Excluding 'Sock It To Me Santa' with The Last Heard some 20 years earlier, this is the nearest Seger ever came to a Christmas record. Other artists contributing seasonal favorites to the album included Eurythmics, U2, Madonna, John Cougar Mellencamp, Alison Moyet, Bruce Springsteen, The Pretenders and The Pointer Sisters. Seger's version reappeared 24 years later on his compilation *Ultimate Hits: Rock And Roll Never Forgets*.

He was also invited to record a new version of Roy Orbison's 'Oh Pretty Woman' to be used as the theme for the Julia Roberts and Richard Gere film of that title, but due largely to his busy work schedule at the time, it never happened.

The Fire Inside (1991)

Personnel:
Bob Seger: vocals, electric, acoustic and rhythm guitar, piano, electric piano
Kenny Aronoff, Richie Hayward, Russ Kunkel, David Teegarden: drums
Barry Beckett, Jamie Muhoberac: synthesizer
Roy Bittan, Bill Payne, Walt Richmond: piano
Bobby Bruce, Lisa Germano, Richard Greene: violin
Chris Campbell, Bob Glaub, James ('Hutch') Hutchinson, Michael Rhodes, Don Was: bass
Mike Campbell, Joe Walsh: lead guitar
Craig Frost: organ, synthesizer, piano
Bruce Hornsby: piano, accordion
James Newton Howard: Synclavier
Dann Huff: electric and rhythm guitar
John Jorgensen: slide guitar
Steve Lukather, Dean Parks: acoustic and electric guitar
Buell Neidlinger: acoustic bass
Don Potter, Fred Tackett: acoustic guitar
Alto Reed: saxophone
Rick Vito: lead and slide guitar
Waddy Wachtel: acoustic and rhythm guitar
Jai Winding: organ
Sweet Pea Atkinson, Sir Harry Bowens, Rosemary Butler, Mimi Cooper, Laura Creamer, Thornetta Davis, Donny Gerrard, Donald Ray Mitchell, Shaun Murphy, Patty Smyth, J. D. Souther, Oren Waters: backing vocals
Produced by Punch Andrews, Barry Beckett, Bob Seger and Don Was
Release date: 27 August 1991
Highest chart positions: UK: 54, US: 7
Certification: Platinum
Running time: 44.52 (standard); 51.26 (plus bonus tracks)

During the late 1980s, Seger began to plan the next album. The next two releases would still be credited, as the last few had been, to himself and The Silver Bullet Band. Nevertheless, the latter now existed only in name, with Craig Frost on eight of the 12 tracks here, while Chris Campbell and Alto Reed now contributed to a minority of songs alongside the ever-changing roster of outside musicians. Seger could now call upon anyone from a large pool of respected musicians, and among those joining him for the first time included drummer Kenny Aronoff and violinist Lisa Germano, both of whom regularly worked with John Cougar Mellencamp, guitarist Mike Campbell – a founding member of Tom Petty's Heartbreakers and Mudcrutch – Joe Walsh from the Eagles, Steve Lukather from Toto, Patty Smyth and Bruce Hornsby. One of the bassists, as well as one of four producers involved, was Don Was. Seger loved working with him: 'I could just sit back and enjoy him taking the wheel.' In turn, Was said that Seger 'isn't like some sheltered star; he's been out there living. He's had some trauma mixed in with success. He's a frayed soul, and he's a real honest artist. It comes out in his work.'

For *The Fire Inside*, Seger had written 38 songs, recorded over 20, and of these, 12 were chosen for the CD, and ten for the LP. Don Was produced half the record, the rest being shared out by Seger, Andrews and Barry Beckett between them. 'I think it's a nice balance of stuff,' Was said, 'and there's a lot of not typical Seger material.'

It was apparent by now that he released only about half the songs he was recording, with a very small proportion of outtakes ending up as B-sides or giveaways to movie soundtracks. That suggests that he, management and record company were maintaining strict quality control; otherwise, they could still have been releasing another album of new, probably substandard songs every two years or so. Many a less conscientious performer would have probably thought nothing of doing so.

The album still went top ten in America, but the media reaction was lukewarm at best. Andrews commented that the radio stations had wanted another rocker as a single, and when they didn't get one, 'they bitched for three weeks.' Under the heading, 'Bob's fire needs stoking', Steve Hochman wrote in the *Los Angeles Times*, referencing one of his best-loved hits, that 'if all you want is the same old Seger, you got him again, but you might as well just take those old records off the shelf.'

'Take A Chance' 3:41

Had ABBA not laid claim to it 13 years earlier, this song might well have been named 'Take A Chance On Me'. Lyrically, it's more than a little economical on the word front, with the title appearing 33 times from start to finish. As for the tune, it opens on a three-chord intro, C, G, Am, played four times, clings doggedly to the same sequence throughout the song with no instrumental break, then finishes on the sequence repeated four times before an orderly conclusion. The lyric is a fairly abstract one of how you take a chance when you cross the street, love somebody, be honest, tell a lie, trust somebody – or do anything. It's a piece of music that doesn't take a single chance itself and is about as repetitive as 'Happy Birthday', if not more so, as it lasts much longer, but for all that, it's not unenjoyable. The instruments settle with ease into the riff over and over again, and only when the outro comes do they have a chance to break into a sweat for the last four bars.

'The Real Love' 4:40

This was the album's only hit single, released at about the same time as the album and peaking at number 24. It's not startlingly ambitious or adventurous, with its gentle melody given a warm foundation of strings-like synth, backing vocals, acoustic guitar and a few decorative yet unobtrusive little flourishes on guitar and synths. Simple in the extreme, yes, with a carefully-inserted bridge to prevent monotony from creeping in, but it seems a little churlish to find fault with it for that. In his mid-40s, the rocker who used to bring concertgoers in their thousands to their feet with so little effort was growing, well, middle-aged gracefully and with style.

'Sightseeing' 3:39

Three interesting pictures in words from Seger come in the verses of this song: a crumbling, decaying castle, damp and musty; then a tall, blue-eyed redhead in a busy brasserie who catches his eye; and finally, a Yves Tanguy painting in a gallery that appears to be looking back at him. Is this his way of looking back at the past or contemplating his future? It hardly matters, but musically, the song breaks new ground and is one of the album's best tracks. Here, he's heading for folk territory, or more specifically, Cajun. It's a joyous tune with a swing in its step, with Hornsby's accordion and Germano's fiddle leading the way, suggesting that John Cougar Mellencamp's *The Lonesome Jubilee* album (on which both Germano and drummer Kenny Aronoff had also played) may have been on his personal playlist. There's also a lovely touch on the backing vocals part of the way through, which, according to the album notes, feature Gerrard, Souther, Smyth and Seger himself on 'Center vocal chorus'.

Seger hoped that it might have been considered as a single, and as an infectious song in a departure from his usual style, it would probably have been an enterprising move. He was proud of it 'because it's a very odd structure in that the title is in the bridge', but was warned that on broadcasting grounds alone, it would be impossible. 'I've already heard from various radio programmers who tell me that they can't play it because it doesn't fit into any format. I would love to put that as a single just because it's so unique, but I doubt that will happen.'

'Real At The Time' 3:53

This revisits an old relationship, one that seemed 'real at the time' as the choruses remind us over and over again. His love for the 'lioness tall and lean' was soon destroyed by pettiness and fights between a couple of kindred souls fighting for control. Like 'Take A Chance', lyrically it's repetitive and musically rather unadventurous, stuck on a semi guitar-grunge two-note chord sequence for much of the time, apart from a short bridge about 90 seconds in, where two extra chords enhance the tune all too briefly.

'Always In My Heart' 4:14

From the title, you know this is going to be yet another so-so heartfelt love song. There's nothing wrong with that, but then again, there's really nothing to make it stand out from the rest. It's made up of three verses, two of them separated by a bridge, a simple melody built on piano chords with gentle synthesizer adding a little color in the backing, but little else, making this the album's least memorable four minutes.

'The Fire Inside' 5:56

The title track was the second US single, released in November, but it didn't trouble the charts. This being the age of MTV, an official video was made in black and white, and it's this that gives the main clue as to what the song, with its brisk backbeat and catchy, insistent piano hook, is about. People are out on the city streets at night, 'where the latest neon promises are burning bright'. There are 'phony posers with their worn out lines, the tired new money dressed to the nines', all seeking fulfilment in the lure and the bustle of nightlife but failing to find it while they are 'faking the smile, hiding the pain, never satisfied, the fire inside'. Seger had great faith in the song, knowing it was something special. In his words, it was 'a pistol', and they recorded it four times over the space of more than a year in order to get it just right.

Later, he told Steven Wheeler that he had really struggled with the lyrics and worked on them for a long time. What he wanted to convey was the sense of...

> ...trying to maintain your passion, trying to accept the fact that you have passions and trying to be mature enough not to give in to a lot of temptations. So there's always that balancing going on, which delves into the issue of maturity. Where you're trying to keep the passion alive while stepping away from temptation, and that goes for romantic passion and holding on to a passion for life.

Once Don Henley gave it his seal of approval, he was satisfied. The singer and musician whose judgment he respected implicitly was one of the few people he actually listened to, he said, when it came to playing his new songs for others. 'I'm not afraid to make mistakes, but if Henley says 'that's really low-rent', then I'll get rid of it.'

'New Coat Of Paint' (Tom Waits) 3:26 (CD, cassette only)

As with 'Sightseeing', Seger broke musical ground again. The first of two visits to the Tom Waits songbook, this is a glorious, lazy jazz/blues take on a song in which he sings of inviting his lady out so they can take a new coat of paint to the lonesome old town, and 'laugh at that old bloodshot moon in that burgundy sky'. Payne's fingers ripple over the piano keys like a riverside stream, while Hayward's drums, Neidlinger's standup bass and Tackett's acoustic guitar all help create a wonderful homespun atmosphere for Seger's relaxed vocals. This was one of the most surprising tracks on the album, and all the better for that. He was particularly proud of it as it was recorded entirely live in the studio without overdubs.

Payne, former Little Feat pianist, was 'just phenomenal on that cut.' Although Seger had played piano himself on two other tracks on the album, he loved hearing someone else like Payne or Roy Bittan at the instrument, especially when he freely admitted that they were much better than him and 'so much fun to listen to.'

'Which Way' 3:57
A slow-paced blues-rock shuffle driven mostly by Jorgensen's slide guitar and Frost's organ, this scores quite well on the musical front, although the lyrics seem a tad unimaginative. 'Which way you gonna go – run – turn?' opens each verse. Musically, it's another languid song that doesn't really break into top gear, but is likeable enough.

'The Mountain' 6:45
The lyrics of this song have been subject to various interpretations over the years. The most likely one is that the mountain signifies a painful relationship in the past, one to move away from in the hope of finding a better future – 'it looms up dark and ancient, its shadow over me'. It's not only the longest track on the album by some way, but also the nearest to hard rock.

A slow, smoldering piece, it completes a circle in which each member of the 1990s lineup of Eagles has guested on one of Seger's albums, now that Joe Walsh has brought his Fender Telecaster along. To a stately, measured rhythm from Kenny Aronoff on the drums, Walsh adds a couple of weighty, grungy-sounding solos. It may not have the same instant appeal as most of the other songs that share this record, but it stands out as one of the weightiest.

'The Long Way Home' 4:24 (CD, cassette only)
Sometimes there is a fine line to be drawn between blandness and genuine emotion in a love song. This one falls into the latter camp, in looking back on a failed relationship. 'She was the best I ever knew, somehow she drifted away' sums it up. This is the confession of a man coming to terms with the passing years – 'now that I'm older, nights seem much colder'. His piano, Frost's synth and the guitars of Vito and Lukather complement this one to perfection. This song about 'lovers, dreamers and beautiful schemers (who) all take the long way home' may, to some, be just another broken-hearted ballad, but this time it's up there with the best of them.

'Blind Love' (Waits) 4:23
As 'Shame On The Moon' proved a few years earlier, Seger had an eye and indeed a voice for country music. Tom Waits' picturesque tale of a love affair that has gone wrong but may be retrievable fits him like a glove, with charming fiddle from Richard Greene, plus a gentle touch on piano and acoustic guitar. Seger was quite in awe of Waits as a writer, saying that he wasn't as poetic and graceful as either him or Don Henley. 'I think they have an ability that I just don't possess.'

'She Can't Do Anything Wrong' (Bill Davis, Walt Richmond) 3:38
There's nothing like ending on a no-nonsense rock 'n' roll tune. It's another song along the lines of 'Sweet Little Sixteen' or 'Little Queenie', give or take an extra chord or two, as far as the lyrics go, with their tale of a girl attracting plenty of attention on the dance floor. Vito's snarling slide guitar adds a touch of Rolling Stones rawness, while co-writer Richmond, keyboard player with country rock band The Tractors, positively shines on piano. Despite this, it was Seger's least favorite song on the album. 'I like the energy and the band really enjoyed playing it, and it's a fun thing, but I'm not particularly proud of it.'

It's A Mystery (1995)

Personnel:
Bob Seger: vocals, synthesizer, guitar, acoustic guitar, piano, drum machine
Kenny Aronoff, Eddie Bayers, Richie Hayward, Russ Kunkel, Gary Mallaber, Harry Stinson: drums
Roy Bittan: piano
George Bohanon: trombone
Rosemary Butler, Laura Creamer, Donny Gerrard, Shaun Murphy, Julia Waters, Luther Waters, Oren Waters: backing vocals
Chris Campbell, Bob Glaub: bass
Craig Frost: synthesizer, keyboards, electric piano
Tim Mitchell, Fred Tackett, Michael Thompson: guitar
Bill Payne: synthesizer
Alto Reed: saxophone
Rudy Richman: percussion
Tom Roady: maracas
Jeffrey C.J. Vanston: synthesizer, keyboards
Rick Vito: slide guitar
Produced by Bob Seger
Release date: 24 October 1995
Recorded at New River Studios, Fort Lauderdale, Florida; Woodland Digital, Nashville, Tennessee; Conway Studios, Los Angeles, California
Highest chart positions: UK: 76, US: 27
Certification: Gold
Running time: 49:49

By the time he came to prepare the follow-up to *The Fire Inside*, as usual, he had a large pool of new original material from which to choose. From 33 songs, he chose 26 to record. This time, he aimed to make what he called 'a big, tough, heavy, rock record' that sounded live 'instead of going for the gloss.' The three remaining members of The Silver Bullet Band were called into the studio alongside a large cast of outside musicians to record what would be the last album credited to The Silver Bullet Band alongside the singer. As usual, he said afterwards that 'the bullets' had a problem with his ballads because 'these guys are real rockers.' The session players would therefore be used mainly for the slower songs.

For the first time, he was credited as sole producer, partly because he intended to complete the job more quickly: 'I wanted to get home to the kids.' It was his intention to aim for a more raw approach this time; he wasn't sure if it was the right thing to do, he told Steven Wheeler, 'but it's my decision and I'll take all the blame or credit this time around.' Significantly, though he was producing himself on his own, he had started to collaborate as a writer. He had never previously felt the need, he said, but now he was working with two of the musicians, keyboard player Craig Frost, who had been part of The Silver

Bullet Band since the 1980 tours, and newer guitarist Tim Mitchell. 'What they do is write these big powerhouse rock grooves, and they send them to me. We all get together and put chords to those grooves and come up with a song.' Some were rejected, but three of their joint efforts passed the test.

To these ears, it sounds like an uneven collection, a few definite below-par items rubbing shoulders with the better ones. One initial listen from start to end gives the feeling that different tracks have been taken from very different sessions, maybe months apart, and the impression is of sonic patchwork, somehow lacking unity. A few years later, he called it his 'garage rock album'. He admitted that he knew he would lose some of his followers because it was a very different album for him. 'I used to write about relationships, and now, with the kids, I'm writing about national problems.' At times, he sounds angry about the state of the nation, but there is still room for moments of charm. Oddly, most of the better tracks appear towards the end of the album. Why some of the weakest had been placed earlier on is indeed something of a mystery.

Early reaction to the record suggested that it was not well-received by his usual public, or even the media. He told the *Detroit Free Press* that 'it might crawl its way to platinum in the next six months, but I knew it was going to be hard to get airplay. I knew the only way to sell it would be to go on tour.' The only radio exposure he was getting was for the old material on classic rock radio, which had just been given a new lease of life with the recent *Greatest Hits* album: 'it's just not the way it was in the old days.' A few business insiders thought that the new record had followed the hits collection too soon. Some years later, a *Classic Rock* 'worst to best' placed this album just one from the bottom, above the barely remembered *Noah*, describing it as 'dulled by flat production and cuts that don't bear the bite and fire of his 1970s classics.'

Like many another act or group who were now regarded as purveyors of 'classic rock', he was realizing that nothing lasts forever, and that to rely on a fanbase who were growing to middle age and beyond was unwise. After almost 20 years of one consecutive top ten album after another in the US, it could manage no better than number 27 at home. When the management sent a copy of the album to MTV with an offer to make a video for any song they wanted, they responded that 'we're not going to play any of it.' His second contract with Capitol was now completed, and his future as a recording artist must have looked a little uncertain.

His last tour had been in 1990. In January 1996, the band were back on the road with the *It's A Mystery Tour*, comprising 64 dates in the US and one in Canada, coming full circle in July. Ticket sales were still strong, and 'Hands In The Air' crept into the national rock singles chart, but the record still failed to go platinum, unlike its predecessors. Reviewing a show in the *Washington Post*, Mike Joyce noted that although he was now a family man of 50, 'he still knows how to make a crowd jump to its feet and scream for more.'

Even more presciently, he went on, 'He wisely played down his current and mediocre album – the new tunes were strictly filler.'

'Rite Of Passage' 3:51
Seger seems to be looking at his homeland and not much liking what he sees. 'It's the age of reason for the anarchist', he sings at the start, then takes us to a rite of passage through a hurricane, making a journey through difficult times to a higher ground, to a brighter light, to a promised land. Biblical references abound at one point – the shriek of Abel, the cry of Cain, and then Abraham taking his son. Lyrically, it's open to several interpretations, though at one stage he dropped hints that it had some bearing on the Gulf War in the early 1990s. Musically, it's built on a powerful wall of sound with gospel-like backing vocals almost as high up in the mix as Seger's own. There's a simple riff running through the whole song, from which it deviates but little. Showcasing a relentless, solid wall of sound, with what comes across as a rather muddy mix with heavy grunge guitars and saxes competing to be heard against a solid wallop from the drum machines, and also Seger himself on synth, it's a noticeable departure from his usual style.

'Lock And Load' (Craig Frost, Tim Mitchell, Seger) 4:55
After that strange wall of sound, the sonic clarity on this song makes a refreshing change. Crashing guitar chords at the start and a steady punch from the drums put this on a firm footing from the start. The title, a firearms metaphor, fronts a lyric that suggests encouragement to get ready for action:

> Time to lock and load, time to get control
> Time to search the soul, and start again

Whether it's a clarion call to revolution, or just a wake-up call to those who have hit rock bottom to take responsibility for themselves and get their lives together, or just a statement of sorts about gun control or lack of it, is up to the listener. Considering the darkness of the subject matter, it's a little surprising that this number was the most successful single. In the US, it reached number 22 on the *Billboard* Rock chart, and number 57 in the UK, his final chart entry in the latter territory.

'By The River' 3:26
This time, there's a relative feeling of calm and peace. It's a return to the more folksy, country mood of songs like 'Fire Lake' and 'Shame On The Moon'. There's nothing very deep here, just the ambience of getting back to nature, strolling by the water, reassured by the rhythm and order of life, a sense of innocence and permanence. Explaining such simple lyrics may seem a little naïve on paper, but after the sense of turbulence from the first two songs, listening to something as gentle as this seems to transport us to another

world entirely. The instrumentation is quite simple, basically acoustic guitar and drums, with a jaunty piano break followed towards the end by sax. The gospel backing vocals add another pleasant touch.

'Manhattan' 5:22
The album's certainly anything but predictable. A sweet song that's almost a lullaby is followed by a dark, gritty number about 'Shakey Jakey', a young man in Manhattan, NYC, whose life seems to revolve around liquor store robberies to finance his next fix. It's been suggested, without much evidence, that the song is actually about the death of Kurt Cobain. Over a verse structure that uses just three chords, plus a brief interlude that introduces an additional minor chord, there's a dense backing track built up mainly of piano, drums and crunchy electric guitar chords. Seger's vocals are not so much sung as growled, in a style similar to Leonard Cohen on his last works after his singing voice had surrendered to the ravages of advancing years. It's generally reckoned to be the darkest number he ever released.

'I Wonder' 4:06
Occasionally, Seger's ballads border on the insubstantial, with little to the melody or the lyrics. Sirius, we assume the star, is shining down on the harbor lights. A boat comes in with the moon across the bay, lighting his journey, and what's it like out there beyond the harbor lights? Dreamlike, ever so gentle, drums, piano and synth – but it's so unfocused that it seems to tell us barely anything.

'It's A Mystery' 4:18
So many things in life are a mystery. Some of the lyrics read almost like a child's book of knowledge. It's a mystery, they tell us, how the sun shines, how our eyes meet, how we keep from sinking under and how all the nonsense set before us is supposed to shock us, but it bores us. Honestly, it's getting to the stage where the verses of some of these songs come across as word games that don't really mean much. The track's saving grace is that the guitar does rock quite hard, particularly in one short break early on, and later in the extended break that finishes the song. But sadly, there's nothing much more to it than that.

'Revisionism Street' (Frost, Mitchell, Seger) 3:48
Let the main writer sum it up in his own words: "Revisionism Street' is angry and hostile in its subject matter, berating people like Kitty Kelly and Albert Goldman – revisionist authors who just do it for the buck.' Interestingly, he himself never became the butt of these muckrakers, choosing as he did to keep his private life away from the invasiveness of the gutter press. In the song, Revisionism Street is a place where nobody's memory is sacred, where it's the sleaze-hounds' business to 'dig up something really nasty'. While a

tree falls in the forest and a million copies go to print, 'some parasitic little feeder sits back and makes a mint'. Again, the vocals are largely spoken rather than sung. Once more, instrumentally, it sounds too mechanical with the omnipresent drum machine, and there's little tune or anything in the way of a hook to speak of, but appropriately enough, Mitchell's guitar snarls quite viciously.

'Golden Boy' (2:25)
Is this a song dedicated to Seger's son, rather like 'In Your Time'? Or is he addressing a talented youngster, a prodigy who has everything in the way of adoration, talent and even fame, who is reminded to keep his feet on the ground, to stay true to himself and not become another child star? It's another of those pleasingly simple songs, but with just Seger's vocal, his own ethereal synth and a drum machine behind him, it sounds more like a demo in need of further embellishment.

'I Can't Save You Angeline' (3:56)
In which Seger sits down at the piano and addresses Angeline, a wild child and party animal from whom he needs to break free. He was a rolling stone, but now he's hanging up the guns and walking away from her endless party scene, the weekend warriors' dream. We are presented with three fairly short verses and an even shorter interlude on a song best described as a mid-tempo blues shuffle. Slightly sped up, it would have been perfect for Status Quo. It's uncomplicated, it's not addressing the evils of the present world, and after several of the preceding tracks, it comes as a touch of more than welcome light relief. The addition of a belting guitar solo would really have been the icing on the cake, but one can't have everything.

'16 Shells From A Thirty-Ought Six' (Tom Waits) 4:20
Seger's next journey to the Tom Waits songbook is this charmingly eccentric narrative, the original of which appeared on the latter's 1983 album *Swordfishtrombones*. The narrator has caught a black crow in a Washburn guitar, bangs on the strings to drive him crazy and strums it loud to rattle his cage. He also makes a ladder from a marimba, beats a French horn into a billy can and then blows a hole in the sky the size of a kick drum. Owning a Thirty-Ought-Six, a 30-06 Springfield rifle cartridge, evidently turns you into a madman. The song had started life about six years previously, about a farmer who shot 16 shells into a scarecrow out of sheer frustration during a prolonged drought.

Seger follows the arrangement of the original quite closely, although naturally Waits never had that marvelously gravelly rasp to his voice. Yet it's only this version that makes it clear that the verses are almost a 12-bar blues in disguise. Tackett's marvelously bombastic guitar chords and Zito's exemplary slide work shine, and like the original, everything cuts out towards the fade at the end except for drums. It's not the last Waits song that Seger would record, and he could have done many worse things than offer the world a complete album of 'Seger Sings Waits'.

'West Of The Moon' 4:37

Seger loved his ballads by this time, and there's a fine line to be trodden between charm and utter blandness. This is one of his loveliest, a hymn to the mountains that lie west of the moon. Beneath the sky, eagles soar, horses run free, there's not a care in the world. The melody really takes flight at the bridge, with a powerful yet still sweet guitar solo. The song ends with a couple of lines sung softly, where everything cuts out behind him but the piano, which introduces a brief minor chord that makes all the difference.

'Hands In The Air' (Frost, Mitchell, Seger) 4:45

Before you think the man is mellowing out, on the album's last song, he gets angry again. The world is full of two-time losers, death wish addicts, corrupters of truth, killers of spirit, marauders of youth, and the guilty need to stand up and be counted. The guitar rocks viciously on this angry mid-tempo rocker, though it sounds like the drum machine is still around instead of a good-spirited human beating all hell out of the skins and the cymbals. Despite that, after some of the patchy, if not frankly disappointing, tracks that preceded it, this is not a bad way to close the album.

Face The Promise (2006)

Personnel:
Bob Seger: vocals, synthesizer, percussion, electric and acoustic guitars
Bernie Barlow, Bekka Bramlett, Laura Creamer, Thornetta Davis, Leslie Mills, Shaun Murphy: backing vocals
Eddie Bayers, Steve Brewster, Paul Leim: drums
David Cole: percussion
J. T. Corenflos: electric and acoustic guitars
Eric Darken: tambourine
Kenny Greenberg, Brent Rowan, Biff Watson, Marlin Young: electric guitar
Aubrey Hayne: fiddle
Steve Herman: trumpet
Jim Hoke, Randy Leago: tenor saxophone
William Huber: trombone
John Jarvis, Gordon Mote, Steve Nathan, Bill Payne: piano
Sam Levine: baritone saxophone
Patty Loveless: duet vocal
Larry Paxton, Michael Rhodes, Glenn Worf: bass
Kid Rock: electric guitar, duet vocal
Strings: David Angell, Zeneba Bowers, John Catchings, David Davidson, Conni Ellisor, Carl Gorodetzky, Jim Grosjean, Craig Nelson, Carole Rabinowitz, Pamela Sixfin, Elisabeth Small, Gary Vanosdale, Mary Kathryn Vanosdale, Matthew Walker
Produced by Bob Seger, except 'Real Mean Bottle', produced by Seger and Kid Rock
Release date: 12 September 2006
Recorded at Ocean Way, Nashville
Highest chart positions: UK: did not chart, US: 4
Certification: Platinum
Running time: 42:25 (standard); 45.22 (plus bonus track)

In March 2004, recognition of Seger's achievements came when he was inducted into the Rock and Roll Hall of Fame. Kid Rock, a fellow performer from the younger generation (also managed by Andrews), and a lifelong fan, introduced the man he called 'the most underrated singer-songwriter and live performer of our time.' In his acceptance speech, the latter thanked Punch Andrews, The Silver Bullet Band, his wife and children, and others who had been instrumental in his career. Bringing the band back on stage, they played 'Old Time Rock And Roll' and 'Turn The Page'.

By then, it was known that he was working on another new record, due for release later that year. His contract with Capitol had been renewed, and it would have boded ill for his reputation if the final new release of his career had been the lame, underperforming *It's A Mystery*. He might have been aware that it was time to win back the audience that had felt the previous record fall short of his high standards, and he was hard at work choosing from the songs he had available: 'You've got to get a standard bearer, something you want the album to stand up to.'

Fans would have to wait another year for the results, which followed a brief outside collaboration. In 2005, he made an appearance on record with US alternative rock band 3 Doors Down, and was duly credited as guest vocalist on *Landing In London*. A single from the album, 'Seventeen Days', reached number 56 on the *Billboard* chart in the summer of 2005. Seger's record was further delayed when he and the band went back on tour with 24 dates between February and December 2006, and a further 31 between January and March 2007. It would, however, be well worth the wait, and it became his first to reach the top five since *Like A Rock*. It was also the first credited to him alone, without The Silver Bullet Band, since *Beautiful Loser* 40 years earlier, and also the only one so far never released on vinyl. When it appeared, there was some doubt as to whether it would be his swan song. As he commented later, he'd had a great career: 'I don't know how much more there is to prove.'

'Wreck This Heart' 3:53

First of all, instead of the muddy, grungy sound that opens track one on *It's A Mystery*, this kicks off proceedings with a good, clear sound, snarling rhythm guitar and a proper kick on the drums instead of that metronomic bash from the drum machine. It's a real tonic for the ears to hear someone hitting those skins and cymbals. As for the song, it's about weariness and the onset of a harsh winter storm in Michigan, about working too hard, missing the wife, kids and dog. So, he decides, let's 'wreck this heart' and break free of the grind of it all. Moreover, there's a good little hook in the chorus, not to mention the little boost it gets from the backing vocals. Vintage Rolling Stones meets Bad Company, almost, and it beats nearly everything on the last studio album.

'Wait For Me' 3:42

Love ballads have long since been a staple part of Seger's repertoire, on each album, but for all their sincerity, sometimes they end up sounding too facile or superficial, particularly the lyrics. There are shades of 'Against The Wind' on this one, but this is less of a country song, boasting as it does a more gritty guitar solo, and there's more depth in what he has to say.

'Face The Promise' 3:18

In Seger's words, the title track is a 'big, storming rocker'. The lyrics tell of someone who's had enough of back-breaking work and is in pursuit of a better future in the Promised Land. He's 'small towned out', needs city lights and a wheel in his hands – and at last intends to be his own boss. A powerful beat and guitars, plus full-blooded backing vocals, give this one plenty of flavor. There's something of the no-nonsense guitar, drums and occasional synths wall of sound to this and several of the other songs that had characterized ZZ Top's style during the mid-1980s, their most successful era.

'No Matter Who You Are' 3:40
A song with warnings in almost every line about life's harsher lessons, this could perhaps be some friendly paternal advice to growing children. No matter what you are, the basic theme goes, there's always going to be someone making demands of you. The most chilling line, perhaps, is 'Discover something pure then sit and watch it die'. There's a whole world between 'the soaring dreams and the bottom line'. Another mid-tempo rocker with a powerful rhythm guitar running through it, again, the gospel-like backing vocals do it full justice.

'Are You' 3:35
Here comes another of life's great lessons, and this one comes across as a warning about greed and how it doesn't solve everything. Everyone is on a never-ending quest, setting themselves foolish, impossible goals – the world will make you crazy if you never have enough. Seger sounds quite angry on this one, a message again driven home by fierce, uncompromising guitar.

'Simplicity' 3:59
At this point, it becomes apparent that there's a thread running through these tracks, a kind of life skills programme. 'Keep it simple stupid' might almost have been the title here. 'Simplicity, it works for me', runs the opening line. 'I focus on the basic stuff, so much clutter clouds our way.' With a lyric that's fairly solid without being too complex or too superficial, there's a robust backing of gutsy backing vocals, gritty guitar and an insistent horn riff reminiscent of Stevie Wonder's 'Superstition', and a style that suggests the rock-funk crossover, which began with The Doobie Brothers' golden era in the mid-1970s, plus tracks like Climax Blues Band's 'Couldn't Get It Right' and Wild Cherry's 'Play That Funky Music'.

'No More' 2:58
If anyone still doubts that Seger had really returned with a quality album, this should dispel them. In his younger days, he had been singing passionately about, and indeed against, the war in Vietnam. By the time he had reached 60, only the location had changed, and now the battlefield was Iraq. The emotion and the anger, still proving he can hit those high notes, are evident in the lyrics of this song:

> It was 40 years ago and I was young
> And the jungle not the desert heard the guns
> Someone said they had a secret plan
> And the rest of us were told to understand

Well I don't want this, no I don't want this
I have had enough, no more.

The arrangement also includes a string collection, giving it everything without overwhelming the simplicity and feeling of it all. A touch under three minutes long, you're left with a longing for it to continue a little longer. It's arguably the high point of the album.

'Real Mean Bottle' (Vince Gill) (with Kid Rock) 3:05
The only non-original song on the album is a track written by country singer and guitarist Vince Gill. He penned it as a kind of tribute to country greats like Merle Haggard (referenced in the lyrics as 'Hag') and Johnny Paycheck. 'Hag' had always been a hero of his, especially since they had briefly met around 1980, not long after one of Gill's early songs, 'I'm Almost Ready', had been recorded by Haggard's (then) wife, Lenora. The initial inspiration for this song and title came after a conversation Gill had with veteran guitarist Harold Bradley. The latter had told him about a session he recorded with Hank Williams Sr, and after playing one song together, he said that it might have been the saddest song he'd ever heard. Williams, who had become an alcoholic partly to ease his chronic back pain problem, told him, 'That was a real mean bottle that wrote that song.'

Despite the song's somber history, the performance you hear is a joyous, utterly infectious three minutes of country meets rock 'n' roll, with Seger and Kid Rock cheerfully trading lines. Had the song been written a few years earlier, with its lively guitar solo and piano, it would have been a perfect fit for the likes of Dave Edmunds and Rockpile. There would later be another connection, in that Gill, who had had a successful career in country music for some time, would join the Eagles for their last few post-recording years as a touring band in 2017 after the death of Seger's lifelong comrade in arms, Glenn Frey, as did Glenn's son, Deacon, as an additional guitarist and joint lead vocalist, often singing the same numbers on stage as his father had.

'Won't Stop' 3:19
Maybe it's a coincidence, maybe not, that a song about Merle Haggard should be followed by one about substance abuse and addiction. You can drink all you want, but you won't stop there: 'One day you're a comet, the next day you're dust'. A mid-tempo to slow waltz, it's written as if addressing a friend to help him/herself to break free from the demons. Acoustic guitar and drums provide most of the backing, with a couple of brief but incisive lead guitar breaks.

'Between' 4:48
With an eye on the kind of world his young children would inherit, on this song, Seger addresses the state of the planet, and manages to do it in a

practical, level-headed, non-preachy manner. Lines like 'The world keeps getting hotter, ice falls in the sea, we buy a bigger engine and say it isn't me' and 'We're facing an extinction every other day' make his concerns clear. It's set to a slowish heavy funk rhythm, similar to Bowie's 'Fame', and again there's some fine seething guitar afoot between the verses. The environmental theme was one that he would return to on the following album.

'The Answer's In The Question' (with Patty Loveless) 3:41
If you're recording in Nashville, then there's bound to be not only a country song or two, but also a country duet, with both singers trading lines to good effect. A charming, slow waltz, with lovely fiddle work filling in the spaces, suits this sweet and sour song about the breakdown of trust between a couple. She is coming home late, and her partner begs her 'to leave this all behind'.

'The Long Goodbye' 3:07
The appropriately-titled final song on the original album is a gentle folk number, just Seger and an acoustic guitar, bidding farewell to a partner whom he admits he no longer understands – 'You've become a mystery, will I earn your honesty?' They are about to travel separate roads and carry different loads, with perhaps the saddest line, 'I look into your restless eyes, you turn away, it's no surprise'. A mournful, heartfelt piece that brings it all to a fitting conclusion.

'Red Eye To Memphis' (iTunes bonus track) 2:57
Seger had hesitated about adding this to the album, and perhaps rightly so, as it does sound as if cut from a different cloth than the other songs. There's nothing remotely country here, and in his words, it was 'an almost Tony Joe White thing, a very Memphis-y, fuzzy, R&B country-rock thing.' The swamp rock style suits his vocal, and there's a hit of early Creedence Clearwater Revival in a more laid-back mode. A 'red eye to Memphis' generally means a late-night flight, causing tired, bloodshot eyes, often symbolizing a difficult journey or escape. There's also something of a storyline in these lyrics, although not clearly explained, suggesting an imminent, maybe clandestine rendezvous with a loved one, set to a slow bluesy feel with two lead guitars complementing each other.

Guest Spots

In between his own projects and tours, there was occasional time to make guest appearances on albums by other artists. In 2008, he and country singer Brad Paisley were among the guest musicians who played on a new album by Little Feat, *Join The Band*, which included reworkings of favorites from their back catalogue as well as covers of songs like 'See You Later Alligator', 'This Land Is Your Land' and 'The Weight'. Seger and Paisley sang and played on 'Something In The Water'.

Five years later, he joined John Fogerty on the album *Wrote A Song For Everyone* (Vanguard, US: 3, UK: 75), one of several collaborations with other artists on Fogerty's old songs. They are heard on a duet of 'Who'll Stop The Rain', the song he had written after Creedence Clearwater Revival had played at a very wet and muddy Woodstock Festival in 1969. Both men were much the same age, Fogerty being three weeks younger. Hearing two of America's greatest voices of their time is a sheer pleasure, both taking it in turns to sing individual lines and harmonies on the title phrase. They take it a little more slowly than the band's original, and the additional piano and organ add an extra sparkle without sweetening it, especially on the brief interlude between the second and third verses. The longer coda this time around replaces the shorter one, which faded out Creedence's version, and at 3:12, with a conclusive ending, makes it about 40 seconds longer.

In 2010, Seger's protégé from Detroit, Kid Rock, recorded the album *Born Free* and asked him to play piano on one song, 'Collide'. To Rock's disappointment, he received no reply until a couple of days later when Seger appeared unannounced at the studio. 'Bob, why didn't you call?' he asked. 'I didn't think you were going to do it!' 'I was practising', Seger replied. Sheryl Crow appeared on the same number, on joint lead vocal.

Ride Out (2014)

Personnel:
Bob Seger: vocals, acoustic guitar, banjo, electric baritone guitar, banjo
Eddie Bayers, Chad Cromwell: drums
Jim 'Moose' Brown: B3 organ, mandolin, harmonium, piano, synth strings, synthesizer, accordion
Tom Bukovac: electric, acoustic and acoustic 12-string guitar
Mark Byerly: trumpet
J. T. Corenflos: acoustic guitar
Laura Creamer, Shaun Murphy, Barbara Payton: backing vocals
Eric Darken: percussion
Glen Duncan: banjo
Vince Gill: harmony vocal
Kenny Greenberg: electric guitar
John Jarvis: synthesizer
Bob Jensen: trumpet
Keith Kaminski: saxophone
Rob McNelley: 6 and 12 string, acoustic, electric and slide guitar
Gordon Mote: piano
Deanie Richardson: violin
John Rutherford: trombone
Rick Vito: slide guitar
Biff Watson: rhythm and acoustic guitar
Glenn Worf: bass
Reese Wynans: accordion, B3 organ
String orchestrator: Kristin Wilkinson
Strings: David Angell, Monisa Angell, Janet Askey, Zeneba Bowers, David Davidson, Conni Ellisor, Carl Gorodetzky, Jim Grosjean, Anthony Lamarchina, Carolyn Huebl, Kathryn Plummer, Carole Rabinowitz, Eberhard Ramm, Joel Reist, Sarighan Reist, Elizabeth Small, Elizabeth Stewart, Julie Tanner, Alan Umstead, Catherine Umstead, Gary Vanosdale, Mary Kathryn Vanosdale, Karen Winkelmann
Produced by Bob Seger, except 'All Of The Roads', produced by Seger and Kid Rock
Release date: 14 October 2014
Recorded at Ocean Way, Ben's Studio, Blackbird Studio, all Nashville
Highest chart positions: UK: did not chart, US: 3
Running time: 34:31 (standard); 43:46 (deluxe); 52:15 (Target deluxe)

Though he had already suggested that he had nothing left to prove, by the time he reached his 60th year, he still had two new albums to come, both of them up to standard. In January 2012, after a period of intensive touring, he began writing new songs in earnest for what would become *Ride Out*. At one stage, he said, he had more than 70 to choose from. After touring again for the first few months of 2013, he returned to working, and the album was

completed for release the following year. It was a thoroughly solid collection that sounds like the man is enjoying himself, yet anxious to make sure he doesn't let his fans down by churning out product that he could have made in his sleep. Once you've been releasing records for about half a century, you're not desperate to produce your masterwork anymore, as you've already been there and done that – but you can still deliver the goods.

Face The Promise proved that he had not lost his spark. If his penultimate album harked back in a way to the albums he had made on Palladium/ Reprise some 40 years before, made up partly of other people's songs, he still had something to say with several originals on offer, while he could still pay homage to a younger generation of songwriters whose work he had loved.

It also continued to take him further into a country music direction, with the fiddle more prominent in particular. His wife was a great fan of the genre, and he was now listening to it more and more. Another subtle change came as a result of his using a new guitar tuning, DADGAD, that he had learnt from Jim ('Moose') Brown, who had played guitar and other instruments on his recent albums. It had long been in use in folk and Celtic music, and also used by rock musicians on more acoustic-based tracks, such as The Beatles on 'Norwegian Wood' and Led Zeppelin on 'Babe I'm Gonna Leave You'. He used it to write two songs on *Ride Out*, namely 'Gates Of Eden' and 'The Fireman's Talkin''.

As an album made by a man nearing his 70s, aware of his mortality and the importance of speaking up about things that matter 'before it's too late and I can't even get a record deal anymore', its songs deal with issues that affect the state of the world as he sees it, in particular gun culture and climate change, seen through the eyes of a man nearing old age who is rightly concerned at what his children will face during the years ahead. The cover design included a road disappearing into a desert horizon on the front, and a photograph of a chimpanzee on the back, taken by the late Tom Bert, who had also been responsible for the sleeve images on *Beautiful Loser* and *The Distance*. He knew it would make people wonder why. The chimp, he stressed, was man's closest relative in the animal world, and their population was endangered. The message, he said, is 'let's do something about this.' He knew some people would disagree with him, but he felt strongly about addressing such problems. 'There are a lot of culprits in climate change, and everybody's responsible, myself included. Nobody gets a free pass on this one. We've got to change our ways and change them fast.'

Any fears that this new plain-speaking Bob Seger might have alienated his following were soon dispelled. The record debuted at number three, making it his highest-charting album since *Against The Wind* (34 years earlier), and sold 59,000 copies in its first week.

'Detroit Made' (John Hiatt)

The song first appeared on Hiatt's album *Dirty Jeans And Mudslide Hymns* in 2011. He wrote it as an ode to the Buick Electra 225, which was a full-size premium car built by the Buick division of General Motors in Detroit between 1959 and 1990, named thus as it had an overall length of 225 inches. It 'goes like a shootin' star', the lyrics say, and is clearly the vehicle to have.

> Now when I first got out of high school,
> I drove an old fine truck.
> All the girl they walk right by me,
> Didn't even say good luck.
> Now I ride my 225 they all wanna be my friend.

When Seger first heard it, he knew he had to record his own version. Any song that reflected his Motor City automotive heritage was fine by him, so he downloaded it, put it in his car and drove around, singing the harmony parts. 'And, of course, the subject matter's a no-brainer because we all love cars in Michigan.' Hiatt's own version is pretty breathless, but Seger's voice suits the song so much better, and once again the full-on wall of sound with guitars, organ, drums and backing vocals turns the song into a blaze of glory.

'Hey Gypsy' 2:32
Arguably the best track, this is Seger's tribute to Stevie Ray Vaughan, the guitarist tragically killed in a helicopter crash some 14 years earlier, as he was keen to honor his memory and how much he meant to him. It's a rollicking Texas swing-styled 12-bar blues, and to make it sound as authentic as they possibly could, self-confessed fan Seger said he called the players in Nashville and instructed them to play as close to Stevie Ray as they could. 'The guitarist Kenny Greenberg, whom I was working with at the time, brought a special amp in that made him sound exactly like Stevie Ray! We even got Stevie Ray's old organ player, Reese Wynans. That's the first time I used him, and he's on everything [on the album] now.'

'The Devil's Right Hand' (Steve Earle) 3:49
One of Earle's best-known songs had started as a B-side to one of his early, unsuccessful singles, and might have been forgotten had not Waylon Jennings recorded it himself in 1986. His version was subsequently used in the 1988 movie *Betrayed*. Seger was always a big Jennings fan, discovered it while watching the film and decided he would do it himself one day. Only later did he learn its full history. 'Oh my God, Steve Earle wrote it! No wonder I like it!' was his reaction. Several other acts have recorded it since, including Johnny Cash, both as a soloist and with The Highwaymen (Cash, Jennings, Kris Kristofferson and Willie Nelson). It's a powerful critique of gun culture, yet still a catchy song, telling the story of a lad who was obsessed with firearms from childhood, whose mother always said that the pistol was the devil's right hand, and as a young man, ended up in court after shooting a card cheat. Earle and Jennings turn in fine performances, but Seger's recording is

arguably the strongest, with its muscular guitar, sturdy drumming, and above all, shimmering organ.

'Ride Out' 3:07
As a parent of two children approaching adulthood, in the lyrics to this song, Seger takes a measured look at past, present and future with cautious optimism. His message is basically an invitation to 'ride out to a bold new horizon, lift your soul and your spirit, take a chance and get near it, everybody needs a dream'. The world is full of pitfalls, challenges and opportunities. 'Time to disconnect from clutter', he advises, 'time to hit the road'. In another verse, he asks, 'Is the media for real? Do we fake or do we feel?' There's a brisk rhythm on the drums, with a few subtle phrases from the electronic horns punctuating the rhythm guitar-led backing, and sparing use of backing vocals.

'Adam And Eve' (Kasey Chambers, Shaun Nicholson) 3:12
Written, recorded and first released by Australian (then) husband and wife duo Kasey Chambers and Shaun Nicholson on the album *Wreck & Ruin* (2012), the former said that it 'takes a very old traditional type of story and puts a modern twist on it.' On Seger's version, the voice of Eve is taken by Laura Creamer, and the biblical creation tale becomes a duet with paradise, temptation and human frailty the main theme. Some lines feature them combining and harmonizing to perfection. Bass and drums add the lightest touch, supporting Duncan's banjo, Richardson's fiddle and Brown's mandolin and harmonium with flair.

'California Stars' (Woody Guthrie, Jeff Tweedy, Jay Bennett) 4:44
'California Stars' was one in a batch of lyrics from the archives of Woody Guthrie, which he left on his death in 1967. In 1995, Billy Bragg played a Guthrie tribute show in Central Park, NYC. Afterwards, his daughter Nora contacted him with a view to setting them to music, so that they could be passed down to a new generation of musicians to perform and record. Bragg contacted Chicago-based band Wilco to finish some of the songs, which the singer and band recorded together on the album *Mermaid Avenue* (1998).

The album's longest track, it tells of the aspirations and hardships of migrants during the Dust Bowl era of the 1930s, when poverty-stricken families from Texas and Oklahoma dreamed of finding a better life in California, hence the line about a man dreaming all his troubles away as he lays his head on a bed of California stars at night. From a gentle introduction of fiddle and acoustic guitar, maintaining the folk tradition, the accompaniment builds with banjo, piano, and above all, brass, complementing the rhythm section. This is probably one of Seger's finest ventures ever into the country music genre.

'It's Your World' 3:17

Around the time of the album's release, Seger admitted he was increasingly focused on environmental issues, how they would affect his children's generation, 'wanting them to have a future and a good place to live'. Without getting too preachy, in the lyrics to this song, he lays bare his concerns about the planet. 'Say a prayer for the victims of extinction, say another for the redwood trees', he sings. It's important to talk about acid in the ocean, dying coral reefs, mortgaging the future and the underlying problem, 'cash is king'. 'It's your world', the chorus, enhanced by gospel-style backing vocals over the repeated three words, constantly reminds us. It's significant that the instrumental embellishment is kept fairly basic, with an insistent drum pattern throughout alongside a growling rhythm guitar, pounding piano and little else.

'All Of The Roads' 3:34

'All of the roads I've run, all of the faces I've left in my wake', runs the opening line of this gentle, introspective number. There's a hint of underlying mortality as well – 'After the lights the darkness is coming soon'. In part, it's a gentle reflection from a man looking back at his life, hoping to leave his mark, 'hoping I gave and just didn't take'. At the same time, it serves as an acknowledgment of and to the audiences who followed and supported him. He'd done it all before, gone through every door. 'I'm so grateful for the fans, and I just wanted a song to explain what it's like, to tell them I tried my best. And to say: Thank you for coming, and thank you for hanging with me all these years.'

The tune is one of the strongest on the record, and the combination of piano, organ, backing vocals and even a short violin solo is irresistible.

'You Take Me In' 2:33

As already noted, sometimes there's a fine line between a genuinely moving, tender love song and a bland, insubstantial one. This one falls neatly into the former category. Many a singer-songwriter has penned a love letter in music to his or her other half, and here Seger gets it right throughout in his simple, soul-baring tenderness, written for his wife. The guitars, synthesizer and drums are all appropriately gentle, creating the perfect ethereal backdrop for the warm tones of his voice.

'Gates Of Eden' 3:47

The closing song on the standard ten-track version of the album is unconnected with Dylan's song of the same title, although it still deals with the same subject, the Gates of Eden personifying a corrupt world that, contrary to general belief, is not the entry to paradise. Seger sings of a world of disillusion, of a whole day that for him 'had been a journey sorting through the truth and lies', and ultimately an account of spiritual awakening.

I remember searching, longing for a deeper meaning
And it hit me like a diamond bullet, right between the eyes.

Yet everything he reads calls into question everything that he believes in, 'huddled with the masses stranded at the Gates of Eden'. During the early stages of writing, he had reached the chorus, 'I believe'. It made him think carefully about what he really believed. 'I believe that religion is just fine if it helps people find peace, to be good to their fellow man. It's a good tool for living a good life. And I said, well, I never personally really had a spiritual awakening; it's been gradual. But I see my kids and so, yeah: I believe in God.'

It's a slow, majestic song that comes to a false conclusion after two and a half minutes in, and starts again with a minute-long, remarkable orchestral coda that includes a glorious break on McNelley's slide guitar. He said that friends and family told him it was his best work in years, his son telling him that out of all the songs he had written, this was his favorite.

Deluxe Edition Bonus Tracks

'Listen' 3:20

A jaunty, skiffle-folk song backed by acoustic guitar, simple percussion (the singer tapping his foot, maybe?), Wynans' unobtrusive accordion and Vince Gill singing harmony. It sounds like it may have been recorded in one take. The message is very simple – in a busy world of information overload, if you want the truth, 'if you listen you will hear'. Seger wrote it, he said, when it dawned on him and Nita that they were always giving their son and daughter advice and then interrupting them. One day, both parents were sitting on the couch, and their son entered in a really frustrated mood. 'He just wanted to vent, and all we did was sit there and listen – didn't say a thing. And then after he left, what was really strange was that we'd been discussing exactly that before he came in. Sometimes it's a better thing to listen. You never hear the truth if you don't.'

'The Fireman's Talkin'' 2:44

The inspiration for this was provided by wise words from the perspective of Nita Seger's brother-in-law, a professional firefighter. 'What's a good man warning us about?' he asked. 'Someone who rescues people and puts his life on the line? That it could get hotter'. Hence, another stark reminder in song of environmental Armageddon. The ice is melting, the seas are high, the smoke is rising and there's no more time. It's all set to a jaunty up-tempo country rhythm, with prominent banjo and fiddle, plus a mighty crash or two from the drums and rhythm guitar as the song gathers momentum.

'Let The Rivers Run' 3:51

Another charming ballad that falls on the right side of the simplicity line. A gently strummed acoustic guitar, soothing piano, which contributes a short instrumental break before the final chorus, and an epic string arrangement form this delightful tune with its hints of mortality and a peaceful acceptance of what will be, will be, 'while the rivers run'.

A Target exclusive deluxe edition included the above 13 tracks, plus two more.

'It All Goes On' 3:41
A mid-tempo, piano-driven song built mostly around minor chords, with the message that little can be done to change the onward march of progress, for better or for worse. Sometimes, it comes at a cost, as the second verse realizes: 'in an all-out war, someone should expect to bleed'. There will be triumphs, there will be challenges, but life goes on all the same. A short guitar break before the final verse adds a neat little spark.

'Passing Through' 4:48
A jaunty country singalong, its philosophical lyrics attempt to take a look at life but say very little. Still, they offer a gentle line or two of advice:

> I can tell you plenty that you might not need to hear
> Maybe it's a blessing some things are left unclear

I Knew You When (2017)

Personnel:
Bob Seger: vocals, electric and acoustic guitars, piano
Herschel and Terena Boone, Bekka Bramlett, Rosemary Butler, Laura Creamer, Donny Gerrard, Shaun Murphy, Barbara Payton: backing vocals
Jim 'Moose' Brown, Craig Frost, John Jarvis: synthesizer
Tom Bukovac, J. T. Corenflos, Kenny Greenberg, Tim Mitchell: electric guitar
Mark Byerly, Bob Jensen: trumpet
Chris Campbell, Jimmie Lee Sloas, Glenn Worf: bass
John Catchings, Carole Rabinowitz: cello
David Cole: acoustic guitar
Chad Cromwell, Richie Hayward, Greg Morrow: drums
Eric Darken, Gerard Smerek: percussion
Jim Kaatz: guitar
Keith Kaminski, Alto Reed: saxophone
Rob McNelley: electric and acoustic guitar [flamenco]
Steve Nathan: electric organ B3, piano, organ, synthesizer
Bill Payne, Mike Rojas: piano
Deanie Richardson: violin
John Rutherford: trombone
Rick Vito, Biff Watson: acoustic, electric guitar
Reese Wynans: B3 organ
Produced by Bob Seger
Release date: 17 November 2017
Recorded at Ocean Way, Ben's Studio, Blackbird Studio and Woodland Studios, all Nashville; Cville Sound, Detroit
Highest chart positions: UK: did not chart, US: 25
Running time: 40.48 (standard); 50:29 (deluxe)

Seger and the band had maintained a steady touring schedule, and the *Ride Out Tour* between October 2014 and March 2015 comprised another 42 dates in the US. Although he was aware that each set of concerts from now on might be the final one, he dissuaded concert promoters from billing it as a farewell tour to capitalize on ticket sales, saying that it smacked of greed. The importance of his leaving the stage at the right time was constantly on the back of his mind. Once his voice went, he promised, he would be gone as well. Had his music had its time, and should he move out of the way? None of them – The Rolling Stones, the Eagles, Billy Joel, Bruce Springsteen – ever expected it to last this long, but if the demand was still there and they could perform, they would continue. As far as he was concerned, there would be one more new album, and another tour, an unavoidably protracted one, still in the tank.

The 18th album, released when he was 72 and appearing 48 years after his debut, would be his swansong. He had been deeply affected by the loss of the man he affectionately referred to as his 'baby brother', Glenn Frey, who had been ill for several months and died in January 2016. After attending his memorial in Los Angeles, he had the idea of sorting through and listening to some of his older, never-released songs. Some were part of the vast archive that he had written and originally recorded years before. Among them was the one that would become the title track. When he had completed the record, he said that it was part of a healing process for him. He could close the book on his recording career with a genuine sense of achievement.

With the announcement of *I Knew You When* on 22 September 2017, 'Busload Of Faith' was released as the album's first single, although in a digital age where 'singles' were largely standalone tracks supplied as downloads to the media for promotional purposes, rather than physical discs. The original had appeared on Reed's 1989 album *New York*. After making a few minor but significant and fully authorized changes to the lyrics, Seger recorded his version at a Nashville studio session during May 2017 and premiered it with Silver Bullet Band at a Cincinnati concert in September, as part of his *Runaway Train Tour*, which had begun on 24 August. The changes to 'Busload' revealed one or two political points, discreetly handled. He had not finished with the subject yet, for the other cover version on the album was Leonard Cohen's magisterial, thought-provoking epic 'Democracy'.

Reaction to the album was generally favorable, if a little guarded. Perhaps some reviewers felt cautious about passing judgment on a new record from one of the rock veterans that they sensed might be his finale. In *Classic Rock*, Kenneth Corsini remarked that while he felt unable to recommend it as a whole, 'there is more to be interested in here than anything Seger has done in years.'

'Gracile' 2:48

The opening song was inspired by Seger's reading of Chip Walter's *Last Ape Standing*, an account of early hominids (two-footed primate mammals, including humans) and lustful early humans. It would be fun, he thought, to write a song about a man from prehistoric times. The woman who's the object of his attentions is gracile, or very attractive and thin. She walked out of evolution's door and is in control. ('Her Strut' revisited, perhaps?) Musically, it's mid-paced funk meets rock, with the tempo and guitar (mainly rhythm plus lead break) tipping their hat to The Beatles' 'Come Together'.

'Busload Of Faith' (Lou Reed) 4:22

The first of two cover versions on the album was a song originally from Reed's 1989 album *New York*. Seger had always loved the imagery it suggested of a busload of people going to work, probably because they couldn't afford to travel by car. Although he never took a co-writer's credit for his efforts, with the approval of Reed's estate, he adapted part of the song by omitting some negative references to religion, another verse about rape and abortion, and with one eye on coming changes in the political situation, altering the lines from 'You can't depend on any churches, unless there's real estate you want to buy', to the more politically slanted 'You can't depend on the president, unless there's real estate you want to buy'.

It keeps closely to the original arrangement, although the omissions make it about 30 seconds shorter, but turn it into a supercharged, cynical performance worthy of The Rolling Stones and The Who at their best. It also shows that while many of his later songs had made him sound much mellower than he did 40 years ago, this track alone proves that vocally he was still a force to be reckoned with, and betrays no apparent strain when he's reaching for the higher notes.

'The Highway' 3:38

The highway referred to here denotes independence, the freedom for people to follow their own instincts. It's one of the songs inspired by Seger's long association with Frey, and their intentions in earlier days to follow their own instincts, 'to turn the wheel away from every deal until [they] find out what's real'. It's driven by fierce, attacking guitar and drums, reinforced by synths, with something of the spirit of Gary Moore & Phil Lynott's hard-hitting anthem 'Out In The Fields'.

'I Knew You When' 3:53

This was one of the songs that Seger found in his archive after Frey passed away. It had been recorded almost 20 years earlier and was considered for *Face The Promise*. After he had listened to it again, he realized that it sounded faintly like an Eagles song ('Tequila Sunrise', for a start, maybe?) and would make a perfect tribute record for him. Then, next time he saw Cindy Frey, his widow, he asked her if she would object to him doing so. She assured him that it 'would be fine in [his] hands.' A charming, mainly acoustic mid-tempo song with the heartwarming backing vocals and piano, some of its lines suggest that it would have been written equally for a loved one or a faithful long-standing companion, especially the time frame in the first line talking about 'the ancient middle 50s, the closin' 60s', and references to how 'you helped me through my darkest hours, you always were my friend'.

'I'll Remember You' 3:48

Not to be confused with a Dylan song of that title that he had recorded and kept in his archive [see 'Unreleased songs' below], Seger reminds us once again of his gift for and mastery of a first-class ballad. Recorded six years or more earlier and intended for *Ride Out*, this is written to a trusted, long-standing kindred spirit. One can imagine him singing this live in concert and having an audience of thousands swaying as they join in with the straightforward but very effective chorus. Simple chords on piano lead the way, with electric guitar and organ in the backing, and again, the well-fitting gospel-like backing vocals.

'The Sea Inside' 4:14

This impressively weighty slow rocker was also on the *Ride Out* shortlist. In Seger's own words, this is 'very Led Zeppelin' with its dark strings, epic guitar solo and thunderous, almost menacing echoes of the Zep classic 'Kashmir'. Its theme is 'a solace in the emptiness', moving away from earthly things, leaving your past behind you. Some might think that this hints at mortality, but in an interview with *USA Today*, he said that it was about the need to get away 'and go deep inside when figuring out what you're trying to say. The way I do it is I get on a motorcycle and just go for a couple of days. That's the imagery I feel – being out there on the open road, when you just need to be alone and say, 'Okay, here's where I am now. Where do I want to go?" In the lyrics, he sings in the last verse that 'It's time to face the wilderness, and sail the sea inside', as the 50-second coda of guitar and strings brings it to a stirring conclusion.

'Marie' (Craig Frost, Tim Mitchell, Seger) 3:26

The first of two co-written songs on the album, this is a rather dark love ballad that suggests an imminent parting, especially in the closing words. 'I'll follow you down for a while', he sings. 'The mountains will shake, and the stars will explode, and I'll leave with a wave and a smile'. Seger described it as 'like me trying to do Leonard Cohen. It's about seduction. It's about a lot of things, but it's very Cohen-esque – it's very minor key, it's got flamenco guitar, the girls are doing the waltzes in the background.' In addition to that striking drum intro, it's also enhanced by simple piano chords and subtle touches of flamenco guitar. Maybe 'sings' is not the correct word, for he half-speaks the lyrics, adding to the Cohen-esque atmosphere.

'Runaway Train' 4.10

The oldest song on the album was first recorded in 1993 and was to be included on *It's A Mystery*. It's another number that sings about seeking freedom, on a highway doing 90 out of control, roaring through the rain and the dark night, the wind in his hair, and not knowing where he's going. 'Is there a reason why I'm on this road?' he asks at one point. 'Is it random or ordained?' The nightmare scenario is set to a mid-1980s-type ZZ Top pulsed rocker or an echo of *Shakedown*, with long-standing sideman Alto Reed on saxophone.

'Something More' 3:47

Recorded in 2001, this slow, moody ballad follows two lovers, not certain of what they want, or indeed the extent of each other's affections. 'This is decision time, you must either fight or flee', one asks the other. Underpinned by piano, the climax comes with a dramatic guitar and sax passage, and powerful backing vocals.

'Democracy' (Leonard Cohen) 6:32

The much-loved veteran Canadian poet and songwriter rarely ventured into political subjects in his songs, but this number from his album *The Future* soon became one of his most talked-about compositions. The record was released at around the same time as the American presidential election brought Bill Clinton to power, and the song soon attracted several cover versions, from such disparate names as Judy Collins, Status Quo and The Lumineers. Cohen had written it at around the time of the fall of the Berlin Wall, to advance his belief that democracy was unlikely to flourish in the Eastern European territories where communist regimes were collapsing, but there was still room for improvement in the democratic processes of the US. 'It's coming to America first, the cradle of the best and of the worst'. (Some staunch patriots may have wanted 'the worst' omitted). According to various sources, it had been between 50 and 80 verses long before he pared it down to half a dozen for recording purposes. The lyrics were left unaltered, unlike the political landscape, which had seen several different American Presidents take and leave office in the 30-plus years since the song had first appeared in 1992.

As a lifelong admirer of Cohen's music, Seger had always loved it and was motivated into recording it himself shortly after Cohen died in 2016. His version is about 50 seconds shorter and omits the penultimate verse from the original, but otherwise follows the original and its arrangement faithfully, from the instrumentation and martial drumbeat to the backing vocals.

Deluxe Edition Bonus Tracks

'Forward Into The Past' (Mark Chatfield, Frost, Seger) 4.10

This was recorded around 1999, and at one time had been intended as the title track of *Face The Promise*. Whether Seger or 'the suits' had second thoughts about unleashing such a dark song on the public, nobody knows, but it's unfortunate that such an important lyric should have been relegated to the marginal status of a bonus-only track. For it must be one of the hardest-hitting pieces of work in his entire catalogue. In it, he paints a stark picture of the decline of rural life in a rapidly changing world where the old ways of rural life are being relegated to history with no regard for the farmers and custodians of the land, now ruthlessly marginalized by the relentless move towards urbanization and corporate jobs. There are metaphors of a bloodshot moon rising on the cornfield and a rusty axe lying in the farmyard while the farmer is being told by the banks to sell up. He evidently has no place in a world of high finance and billion-dollar mergers, all in the name of progress. Over an insistent backing of growling guitar with a couple of solos, and some neat touches of piano, he has rarely sounded this angry.

'Blue Ridge' 3:50

A song written around 1997 about the Civil War provides the theme of the Blue Ridge Mountains and their historical significance. In three verses, Seger evokes the images of battles, of cannon fire and musket shots, and the enduring history of those who fought for the land. He said he thought it was a good metaphor for what the US was going through at the time he wrote it. 'Have you ever seen the country more divided politically?' he asked. 'It's kind of like a political civil war right now, everybody just divided down the middle.' It's similar in musical approach to 'Sightseeing' from *The Fire Inside*, with a strong Brazilian percussion drumming track (think 'The Obvious Child', Paul Simon) running throughout behind the jaunty piano and some crisp lead guitar.

'Glen Song' 2:49

The shortest song on the album, just two verses long, is a gentle tribute to Glenn Frey. Seger released it for free on his official website on 18 January 2017, the first anniversary of his friend's death. It remembers with affection the man who was young, bold and loved his rock and soul: 'there was no one quite like you'. The accompaniment is kept single, with acoustic guitar, a gentle tap on the drums and, in the second verse, a few strings creeping in. It makes for a heartfelt, restrained conclusion to the album, and indeed to the recording career of the man who fondly remembered the man he called his baby brother – the talented comrade in arms whom he had known and sometimes worked with for over half a century.

The Famous Final Scenes

Had everything gone according to plan, the album's release date on 17 November would have coincided with the final date of the *Runaway Train Tour*, named after the song of that name from the album. In the event, all gigs from 30 September were postponed due to what the press called 'an urgent medical issue with his vertebrae.' Of the 32 scheduled, he had played only 13 so far.

After emergency spinal surgery and a lengthy period of rest and recovery, he returned to the stage in November 2018. His command of the stage and his ability to carry audiences with him remained as sharp as ever. The only noticeable concession to his passing years was a case of having to alter the keys on some songs, as those high notes were beyond him now. His setlist included a good choice of over 20 favorites from his back catalogue, going back as far as 'Ramblin' Gamblin' Man'. One of the most moving songs included towards the end of the set was one he had never recorded, Dylan's 'Forever Young', for which he sat at the piano and sang with the full band, while a giant screen displayed images of recently-departed stars such as Prince, Aretha Franklin, Tom Petty, and last but not least, Glenn Frey. To finish, there were two encores, appropriately including 'Rock And Roll Never Forgets'.

Coinciding with the final US tour dates, a promotional single for US radio – a live version of 'Shakedown' – was supplied to Spotify, Apple Music, YouTube and other platforms for streaming and download in August 2019. There was no accompanying physical release.

With the end of the last show, a 24-song set including two encores, at Wells Fargo Center in Philadelphia on 1 November, Bob Seger officially began his retirement. To quote the title of one song from the second encore, it was 'The Famous Final Scene'. There would be one last brief postscript. In October 2023, he made a short (and unexpected) return to the stage, when he performed at the Country Music Hall of Fame in Nashville for the induction of Patty Loveless, playing her song 'She Drew A Broken Heart', followed by a duet for both with 'The Answer's In The Question'.

Live Albums

'Live' Bullet (1976)

Personnel:

Bob Seger: lead vocals, guitar, piano
Drew Abbott: lead guitar, backing vocals
Alto Reed: tenor, alto and baritone saxophones, percussion, backing vocals
Robyn Robbins: organ, clavinet, Mellotron, piano on 'Katmandu'
Chris Campbell: bass, backing vocals
Charlie Martin: drums, backing vocals, answer vocals on 'Heavy Music', harmony vocals on 'Jody Girl', 'Get Out Of Denver'
Produced by Punch Andrews and Bob Seger
Recorded at Cobo Hall, Detroit, 4-5 September 1975
Release date: April 1976
Highest chart positions: UK: did not chart, US: 34
Certification: 5x Platinum
Running time: 70:40 (vinyl); 73:45 (CD, 2011)
Tracklisting: 'Nutbush City Limits', 'Travelin' Man', 'Beautiful Loser', 'Jody Girl', 'I've Been Working', 'Turn The Page', 'U.M.C. (Upper Middle Class)', 'Bo Diddley Medley', 'Ramblin' Gamblin' Man', 'Katmandu', 'Lookin' Back', 'Get Out Of Denver', 'Let It Rock/Little Queenie' (Chuck Berry)
CD reissue (2011) also includes 'I Feel Like Breaking Up Somebody's Home' (Al Jackson, Jnr., Timothy Matthews), recorded live at the Pontiac Silverdome, 26 June 1976

In the mid-1970s, when not in the studio, Bob Seger and The Silver Bullet Band were rarely off the road with a very demanding live schedule.

> We'd done 265 shows with Silver Bullet from October 1974 to September 1975. We were opening for everybody, and if we weren't opening for somebody, we were doing a bar in between. We just played our brains out. What was cool about Silver Bullet was that everybody wanted to play all the time. They were hungry, and they wanted to make it.

Everyone who saw them on stage agreed that they put on an amazing show night after night. It was inevitable that sooner or later they would release an in-concert album, even if they had yet to prove themselves to Capitol as major singles or album chart contenders. Two sold-out shows they headlined at Cobo Arena, Detroit, in September 1975, with Spirit as the opening act, were recorded. As Seger had said, there was a band just waiting to explode on stage. When the house lights went up and they walked on, the crowd went wild, and equipment had to be rearranged as people were continually trying to get up into the performing area with them.

When Seger and Andrews saw the extraordinary success of Peter Frampton's *Frampton Comes Alive!*, which had been released in January 1976 and topped the US charts for ten weeks, there was no holding them back. 'We're better than that, let's do ours!' was their reaction. 'We were definitely a better live act than we were making records.'

'Live' Bullet, another double album, joined Peter Frampton in the racks across the US and the UK in April 1976, received ecstatic reviews in the national press and this time the word spread far beyond Detroit. It reached number 34 on the *Billboard* chart and went on to sell four million copies. 'Nutbush City Limits' made number 69 as a single, whereas the studio version had been a 45 six months earlier and failed completely. UK chart success still eluded them, but would come in time, even if not on the same scale.

It was the first of nine consecutive albums (two live, seven studio) credited to Bob Seger & The Silver Bullet Band, spanning the leading man's career from 1976 to 1995. All the songs apart from 'Little Queenie', which segued from 'Let It Rock', and the standalone minor hit single 'Lookin' Back', had already appeared on his previous albums. During this performance, Seger introduced each of the band members by name. The first four and 'Katmandu' were from the last studio album, *Beautiful Loser*, which they were promoting at the time. Most of them deviated little from the original recordings, except that 'Katmandu' was about half a minute shorter. The exception was 'Nutbush City Limits', on which he addressed the audience mid-song while the band kept the basic riff going quietly behind him:

> As I told everybody last night, I was reading in *Rolling Stone* where they said, 'Detroit audiences are the greatest rock 'n' roll audiences in the world.' I thought to myself, 'Shit! I've known that for ten years!'

It was also partly down to Seger that other British rock acts took to performing 'Nutbush' live, if not on record. Among them were The KT Bush Band, a pub rock outfit fronted by Kate Bush to give her some live experience before she recorded her first album in 1977, Mungo Jerry, ex-Ten Years After frontman Alvin Lee, and Geordie after Brian Johnson had left them. Johnson also performed the song at his successful audition for AC/DC when they were looking for a replacement for Bon Scott after his sudden death.

There were inevitably changes from the studio versions of the other songs. The most obvious is 'Heavy Music', a very short single which, almost ten years later, becomes an eight-minute jamfest with Alto Reed giving it all he can on sax, while the audience are evidently going crazy and Seger is whipping them up with the invitation that 'if you sing with me a little bit I won't guarantee it, but you might just end up on an album.' He kept his promise. There was a reprise of his only hit single of the 1960s, 'Ramblin' Gamblin' Man', about three minutes long this time, giving Abbott a chance to add some solo guitar. While the original recordings were fine, on stage, they were delivered with passion to an equally passionate audience on their home patch, and it showed.

An unsigned review in *Billboard* commented that 'One of the kings of heavy metal rock and a popular live attraction does an LP of what he does best – a concert.' With half-hearted praise, it added, 'Nothing fancy, but a lot more refined than most of the so-called heavy metal acts [sic]. Seger, in fact, is quite melodic when he chooses to be.' In *Rolling Stone*, Dave Marsh also gave a similarly ambivalent verdict. He considered that most of the songs had been better recorded elsewhere, particularly those from *Beautiful Loser*, and two others were particularly disappointing. Even so, the record had 'the advantage of offering a fairly extensive overview of his history.'

The 2011 reissue addition, the slow bluesy 'I Feel Like Breaking Up Somebody's Home', was a minor hit a few years earlier on two occasions, for Ann Peebles and then Albert King.

'Live' Bullet was the record that elevated Bob Seger from local hero to national name. To return briefly to Marsh's review mentioned above, he noted that 'because of the devotion of the crowd and the desperation of Seger's approach (this is something like his last chance to make it to the top, and he knows it), the album transcends its limitations.' If it had been his last chance, it definitely worked. Ironically, the album that had helped to inspire it, Peter Frampton's *Frampton Comes Alive*, would be the peak of the English guitarist's career. After one successful studio follow-up a year later, his subsequent releases met with diminishing success. For the Detroit singer and his band, his record was the catalyst he needed after years of struggle. '*'Live' Bullet* was such a juggernaut', he said. 'It's just fierce. A fierce album. It was a career record.'

Nine Tonight (1981)

Personnel:
Bob Seger: lead vocals, electric and acoustic guitars, piano on 'We've Got Tonight', lead guitar on 'Her Strut'
Drew Abbott: electric guitar; all guitar solos; acoustic guitar on 'You'll Accomp'ny Me', 'Fire Lake', 'Hollywood Nights', 'Against The Wind'
Chris Campbell: bass, backing vocals
Alto Reed: alto, tenor saxophones, flute on 'We've Got Tonight', organ on 'You'll Accomp'ny Me'
David Teegarden: drums, backing vocals
Craig Frost: piano, organ, clavinet
Shaun Murphy: lead harmony on 'Betty Lou's Gettin' Out Tonight', 'Against The Wind', lead backing vocals, percussion
Kathy Lamb, Colleen Beaton: backing vocals, first half of tour, including Detroit shows
June Tilton, Pam Moore: backing vocals, second half of tour, including Boston shows; percussion
Recorded at Cobo Hall, Detroit, May-July 1980**; Boston Garden, October 1980*
Produced by Bob Seger and Punch Andrews

Release date: 8 September 1981
Highest chart positions: UK: 24, US: 3
Certification: 4x Platinum
Running time: 80:00 (vinyl); 67:21 (CD, 2011)
Tracklisting: 'Nine Tonight'**, 'Tryin' To Live My Life Without You'**, 'You'll Accomp'ny Me'**, 'Hollywood Nights'*, 'Old Time Rock And Roll'**, 'Mainstreet'**, 'Against The Wind'*, 'The Fire Down Below'*, 'Her Strut'**, 'Feel Like A Number'*, 'Fire Lake'*, 'Betty Lou's Gettin' Out Tonight'*, 'We've Got Tonight'*, 'Night Moves'*, 'Rock And Roll Never Forgets'**, 'Let It Rock'**
CD reissue (2011) also includes 'Brave Strangers'** (6:48) and 'Let It Rock'** (8:25 on original album, edited to 5:58 for CD)

In March 1980, Bob Seger and The Silver Bullet Band embarked on their *Against The Wind Tour* of North America and Europe, playing over a hundred dates across the next nine months in the US, Canada, and then the UK, Germany, Sweden, Belgium and the Netherlands. It was a good opportunity to capture them in all their glory on stage and record a second live album, with selections from concerts played that summer at Boston and Detroit. Capitol had suggested that a greatest hits album might be in order after a handful of successful singles, but Seger and the band thought that would be premature and decided another live album would be a good alternative. Recordings from shows in Boston and Detroit were accordingly made for the purpose.

The track 'Nine Tonight' had been recorded for the 1980 movie *Urban Cowboy*, starring John Travolta and Debra Winger, and appeared on the original soundtrack album alongside material by other acts including the Eagles, Anne Murray, Boz Scaggs, Kenny Rogers and The Charlie Daniels Band. Seger had also intended it for *Against The Wind*, but it was not ready in time. An infectious, energetic rocker with guitar and sax solos, and a pulsating bassline from Chris Campbell that recalls his distinctive playing on 'Hollywood Nights', it's the song of a young man getting ready for a night out on his motorbike with a girlfriend, and anticipating the sheer joy of their riding 'out past the edge of town, out where the wind's still racin' free on the heartland'. As a brand new song to any concertgoers who hadn't heard it in the movie or on the album, it went down such a storm on the tour that he felt it would be a good title for the album as well. The live version lasts about 30 seconds longer than its studio counterpart, which has a fadeout ending.

'Tryin' To Live My Life Without You' (Eugene Williams) was originally a minor hit for soul singer Otis Clay in 1973, and subsequently covered on albums by Brinsley Schwarz and Dr Feelgood. 'Alright, you guys feel funky tonight? This is an old Memphis song', Seger calls out at the start. Alto Reed later overdubbed multiple sax parts to the in-concert recording, making it sound more like a soul number. Released as a single in most territories except the UK, it made number five in the US. At least one reviewer has commented with amusement on the lyric, pointing out that it's a little unrealistic for anyone to get through five packs of cigarettes and four or five bottles of wine a day. The second US single from the album, 'Feel Like A Number', reached number 48. As mentioned above, in the UK, the live tracks released as singles were 'Hollywood Nights' and 'We've Got Tonight', rather strangely, as the original studio versions had been minor hits only two or three years previously. Even more odd was the use of 'Brave Strangers', live, as the B-side on both.

Apart from 'Let It Rock', the other tracks are basically a 'Bob Seger Greatest Hits 1976-80 Live'. As with *'Live' Bullet*, there is, on the whole, very little variation in arrangements between the original studio recordings and live performances, although the latter pack a little more punch with the adrenaline of playing directly to a crowd who are clearly loving every moment of what they hear and see.

The band are really on fire, particularly with 'Betty Lou's Gettin' Out Tonight' and 'Old Time Rock And Roll', a song they had little enthusiasm for at first, but at length were converted once they saw the positive reaction every time they played it live. One night while they were touring Europe, he suddenly suggested they should play it. 'And the crowd went nuts', he recalled. 'Then we played it in four or five different places in Germany and got the same reaction every single time. The band started becoming quieter about it.' This in-concert version runs about a minute longer than the original, and the chorus around halfway through, where all instruments apart from drums cut out behind the vocal, provides the right time to get the audience to join in, sing along and clap – even if Seger not surprisingly all but drowns them out.

In *Record Mirror*, Mike Gardner hailed it as 'a double live greatest hits collection which effectively shows why America has clutched his comforting use of rock 'n' roll tradition and nostalgic yearning for a lost youth to their communal bosom.' Some reviewers and journalists thought it lacked the power and ferocity of *'Live' Bullet*, and overall, the band sounded 'somewhat neutered'. The singer agreed, saying that he thought it had been done well and people obviously liked it, 'but if I had to do it over [again], I would never have put that album out.' This might help to explain why, during the rest of his long career, he never put out a third live set.

These two fully sanctioned releases have been supplemented by many unofficial ones on CD. Among these are recordings from stage shows and also radio broadcasts from the 1970s that came to light many years later, most of them containing songs that also appeared on studio albums, plus the occasional exclusive. One worth mentioning is *Ebbots Field*, taken from a live FM broadcast of July 1974, featuring two rarities, 'Gang Bang' and 'Don't Burn Down The Bridge ('Cause You Might Wanna Come Back Across)', an old Albert King blues number. *Live In Montreal*, a July 1977 show released (on vinyl) the following year, and *Radio Chicago 1976*, another FM broadcast that appeared 40 years later, are both notable for including Seger and The Silver Bullet Band's boogie-style version of Led Zeppelin's 'Whole Lotta Love' – sounding like Canned Heat meets early ZZ Top. *Transmission Impossible*, a 2017 three-CD set comprising 47 tracks, includes the Ebbots Field set on one record, plus shows from 1980 and 1983 on the other two. *Live On Retro Rock*, a vinyl album released in 1974, includes 'See Me In The Evening' and J. J. Cale's 'Bringing It Back From Mexico'.

Compilation Albums

The Bob Seger Collection (1979)

Tracklisting: 'Night Moves', 'Main Street', 'Let It Rock', 'Leaning On My Dream', 'Ship Of Fools', 'Still The Same', 'Katmandu', 'Mongrel Too', 'Hollywood Nights', 'Travelin' Man', 'Get Out Of Denver', 'We've Got Tonite'

The first of five official compilations was issued in 1979, only in Australia (where it topped the album chart) and New Zealand, credited to Bob Seger (without The Silver Bullet Band), on LP and cassette. All 12 tracks had been previously issued on albums between 1970 and 1978; the majority, eight, were drawn from the last three Capitol releases. ('Leanin' On My Dream' from *Mongrel* becomes 'Leaning On My Dream'). A single album, it was packaged in a gatefold sleeve with thumbnails of eight of the Capitol LPs shown on the inside centerfold, significantly excluding *Noah* and *Brand New Morning*, yet including the debut *Ramblin' Gamblin' Man*, although no tracks from the latter were featured due to time constraints.

A little strangely, in view of his lengthy career, there would not be another similar 'best of' set until the more universally available *Greatest Hits* 15 years later. The nearest Capitol came to this was *Best Collection (1975-1980)* (1980), a 14-track compilation LP (no cassette) that also included material from the next album, *Against The Wind*, credited to Bob and The Silver Bullet Band, and issued in Japan for promotional use only. Significantly, second-hand copies for sale online are higher for the Japanese release than for the more plentiful Australian one.

Greatest Hits (1994)

Tracklisting: 'Roll Me Away', 'Night Moves', 'Turn The Page [Live]', 'You'll Accomp'ny Me', 'Hollywood Nights', 'Still The Same', 'Old Time Rock And Roll', 'We've Got Tonight', 'Against The Wind', 'Mainstreet', 'The Fire Inside', 'Like A Rock', 'C'est La Vie', 'In Your Time'

Certification: 9x Platinum (US); Gold (UK)

Around this time, Seger and Andrews gave some consideration to a long-overdue album of greatest hits. Seger admitted that they were not really a 'pop' band, despite a handful of top ten successes. Nevertheless, it seemed a logical move. Choosing a short enough list was the hardest part, as initially they had 39 titles, and it took him and Andrews a couple of years to whittle that down to what would fit on one CD. Some people around them suggested it should be a double, but as was the case with *The Distance* a good ten years earlier, that would have meant pricing the final release beyond what the average buyer could afford. At length, they reduced the essential titles to 12, plus the obligatory two extra previously unreleased cuts. Their selection of tracks from previous albums, 'hits plus best of the rest', deliberately omitted the two highest-charting singles, 'Shame On The Moon' and 'Shakedown', both left out on the grounds that Seger said they weren't representative of his sound.

The two new items were 'C'est La Vie' and 'In Your Time'. The latter was a song about his son, Christopher Cole Seger, which had been intended for the next studio album. However, when the hits collection tracklisting was being finalised, he believed that it would be better to have one number 'that says here's where we started, and ['In Your Time'] to say here's where we are today. We've all got kids. We're all grown up. We've all hopefully learned a little wisdom we can pass along.'

For this was not only Seger's first compilation of hits, but also his first record as a father. After two brief and childless marriages, in 1993 he married 'Nita' (Juanita) Dorricott, and they had two children, Christopher and Samantha. Both of them inherited a measure of their father's musical talents and became part of the live band from time to time. As well as becoming a film director and screenwriter, Christopher joined his father on stage on the final tour to play saxophone, while Samantha played tambourine and contributed backing vocals.

The album was released on LP, CD and cassette in October 1994. In the US, first week sales totalled 80,000, and it entered the charts at number eight. On British release in February 1995, two weeks after a reissue of 'We've Got Tonight' had given him his highest-ever UK singles chart position at number 22, the album debuted at number six, his first to make the British top 20. In December 2009, it was confirmed that in its home market, it had outsold The Beatles' *1* and Michael Jackson's *Number Ones*, and become the best-selling US catalogue album of the decade, as well as the best-selling album of Seger's career by a healthy margin. In February 2026, it attained its 600th week on the top 200, thanks mostly to regular streaming on Spotify, Apple Music and other platforms.

As mentioned above, reissues of 'Night Moves' and 'Hollywood Nights' would also enter the UK singles charts, the latter for the second time (or third if the live version is included), although falling short of the top 40, during the months following the album's release.

The front cover shot of Seger with his guitar was taken on the Southern Pacific railroad tracks north of Mojave, California. The artwork also includes a photo by Nita Seger of their son, aged 17 months, as well as photos of Frost, Campbell and Reed with their children. Andrews was not over-enthusiastic about the family album theme idea, but Seger insisted.

'C'est La Vie' '(You Never Can Tell)' (Chuck Berry) 2:58

Most of Chuck's best-loved songs had three chords, but this one needed only two. It was one of several vintage oldies, alongside 'Blue Monday' (used on the soundtrack of *Road House*) and Little Richard's 'Lucille', that they recorded to warm up during early sessions for *The Fire Inside*. As Seger recounted in the booklet notes, they had a lot of fun playing this one, and no overdubs were needed. 'It makes sense to have it on here. It's a lot like what we used to play in the early days, loose and unpolished and rough.' Reed was one of four sax players to be heard, and Frost excelled himself on piano in what is pure good-time rock 'n' roll. This track appeared on the album and as one of two supporting numbers on the top 30 UK CD single of 'We've Got Tonight'.

'In Your Time' 3:05
This was written for Christopher, a charming song that reads rather like a hymn, as appropriate for a father to a young son. It forecast the things that would inevitably happen to or around him one day, such as his innocence falling away, fields of green tumbling through his summer days, massive storms reaching his eastern shores – a gentle warning of what life would hold. Reed's saxophone is a particular treat on this one. It was released as a single in the US early in 1995, but without success.

Greatest Hits 2 (2003)
Tracklisting: 'Understanding', 'The Fire Down Below', 'Her Strut', 'Beautiful Loser', 'Sunspot Baby', 'Katmandu', 'Shame On The Moon', 'Fire Lake', 'Tryin' To Live My Life Without You', 'Shakedown', 'Manhattan', 'New Coat Of Paint', 'Chances Are' [with Martina McBride], 'Rock And Roll Never Forgets', 'Satisfied', 'Tomorrow', 'Turn The Page' [video]
Certification: Gold
After the 1996 tour, Seger put his musical career on hold. With two young children, it was time for him to enjoy the quiet life of a husband and father, largely free from the pressures of show business. He continued to write, but the pressure of getting another album out to a deadline was now a thing of the past, and without another tour scheduled, he could afford to take his time. In order to remind the public that he was still in business, another compilation album was issued.

It was inevitable that a second would follow after a reasonable interval, especially as the two highest-charting singles of his career had been deliberately omitted from the first. The real classics had been on the 1995 *Greatest Hits*, and this justified itself as a tidying-up 'best of the rest' exercise, although this time around, there was less interest. In the US, it peaked at number 23, but failed in the UK.

Alongside a selection of hits and tracks going back to 1975 were bonus tracks, one a country duet, and two recorded with a lineup including Brent Rowan and J. T. Corenflos (guitars), Glenn Worf (bass), Paul Leim (drums) and Steve Nathan (keyboards).

'Chances Are' [with Martina McBride] 4:18
From Hope Floats, original motion picture soundtrack, 1998
Produced by Don Was
A duet with Nashville country singer Martina McBride, this ballad features both singers taking a verse separately and then singing harmony on the chorus. He had written it for his wife, and called it 'a blatant love song.' It

began life at sessions for *The Fire Inside*, but after recording it, he said he would 'wait for the right movie to come along' before putting it on his own album. When it was suggested that he could record it as a duet with McBride, he was delighted, and once they began to work on it together, 'we locked right in.' Although physical release was restricted to a one-track promo CD, it still became a top 30 hit on the *Billboard* Hot Adult Contemporary Tracks chart.

'Satisfied' 3:30

A pleasing slow boogie shuffle with Bill Payne's jaunty piano and some good organ fills from Craig Frost, joining the guitars of Seger and Pete Carr, Russ Kunkel on drums, Chris Campbell on bass and spirited backing vocals from the four Waters siblings, reunited on one of his records for the first time since 'Hollywood Nights'. The song itself starts off as a toe-tapping 12-bar blues until the interlude adds a couple of extra chords into the mix. Lyrically, it's a straightforward love song – 'You are the reason that I was born', each verse ending with the line, 'If I had you babe I'd be satisfied'.

'Tomorrow' 3:39

Seger doffs his garage rock persona again for a fairly laid-back blues tune with his own heavy guitar chords throughout, and an incisive, if all-too-brief, solo from J. T. Corenflos two-thirds of the way through. The other musicians include Glenn Worf on bass, Richie Haywards on drums, Eric Darken on percussion and Shaun Murphy on backing vocals. His lyrics throw out a few messages with a veiled caution about global warming, a theme he would return to on his last albums.

> They say the sun is gonna grow some day,
> It's gonna get real close and burn us all up.
> No more traffic in the street, no more road rage,
> No more pretending, things are real tough

At the end, he reinforces the warning:

> I can't promise you tomorrow,
> No one has the light to lie
> You can beg and steal and borrow,
> It won't save you from the sky

Early Seger, Vol. 1 (2009)

Tracklisting: 'Midnight Rider', 'If I Were A Carpenter', 'Get Out Of Denver', 'Someday', 'U.M.C. (Upper Middle Class)', 'Long Song Comin'', 'Old Time Rock And Roll', 'We've Got Tonight', 'Against The Wind', 'Mainstreet', 'The Fire Inside', 'Like A Rock', 'C'est La Vie', 'In Your Time', 'Star Tonight', 'Gets Ya Pumpin'', 'Wildfire', 'Days When The Rain Would Come'

This was what looked at the time like being the first in a series of material from the archives, similar to Bob Dylan's *The Bootleg Collection* that Columbia began releasing in 1991. Its lack of chart success may explain why there was never a Volume 2. It was initially planned as a 'best of' package from the three Palladium 1972-1974 records, until Seger decided to include previously unreleased songs as well, selecting about a dozen and then choosing his favorite four. The numbers appearing for the first time included 'Wildfire', 'Star Tonight' and 'Days When The Rain Would Come', all written in the early-mid 1980s, as possibilities for the album that was to be called *Wildfire* and subsequently became *Like A Rock*. (Their more recent vintage makes the 'Early' title a little misleading). The original tapes for each had fresh vocals, horns and/or other new instrumentation recorded in September 2009 at Kid Rock's studio, Detroit.

As for the older numbers, 'Midnight Rider' from *Back In '72* was now on CD for the first time. 'Get Out Of Denver' and 'U.M.C.' had been available in the early 1990s but were soon withdrawn. They were now remastered and/or remixed, some with new overdubs, at Yessian Studios in Farmington Hills, Michigan, and Kid Rock's Allen Roadhouse Studio in Clarkston, Michigan, in September and October 2009. The Motor City Horns, a Detroit-based horn section with whom Seger had worked before, added horn arrangements to 'Long Song Comin'', a re-recorded version of the song on *Seven*. A new guitar solo by Jim Carty of Mitch Ryder's Detroit Wheels was added to 'Get Out Of Denver', from the same album. Two members of Kid Rock's Twisted Brown Trucker Band, guitarist Marlon Young and keyboard player Jimmie Bones, also played on the sessions.

'Star Tonight' 3:40

Having recorded this for possible inclusion on *Like A Rock*, Seger then passed it to Don Johnson, who recorded it using the same arrangement on his debut solo album *Heartbeat* the following year, with Willie Nelson on backing vocals. It's a rather charming, attractive song about an actress who is indeed going to 'star tonight', presumably on the stage. He sings in his most tender voice, while piano, organ and guitars provide an appropriately gentle accompaniment. Just over halfway through comes a brief but incisive guitar break, all the more powerful as a contrast to the soft instrumentation throughout the rest of the song.

'Gets Ya Pumpin'' 4:09

Recorded initially as 'Pumpin'' in 1973, intended for the *Seven* album, and revisited in 1977, this has all the hallmarks of Seger's early work, and wouldn't have sounded out of place on any album of that period. Like 'Heavy Music', it's a groove rather than a song. The lyrics basically amount to the title, and 'It makes ya feel good, all night long', with Seger hollering close to the top of his range. At the same time, it's an infectious number that sounds like guitar, sax and piano probably made up at a jamming session while he just sang the first phrases that came into his head. Much of the atmosphere comes from the presence of The Motor City Horns, with a sax solo supplied by one of their players, Keith Kaminski.

'Wildfire' 4:37

This song was intended as the title track for what would become *Like A Rock*, but failed to make the final track shortlist. The lads are out cruising, 'with a full moon rising high on a windswept summer night', then they walk into a bar, one of them makes eye contact with the girl with the light blue eyes – and he's smitten, as she shoots through his heart 'like wildfire'. With a strong beat, a short but wonderful guitar solo, and above all, a memorable piano figure running right through, it's an instantly infectious number that makes you wonder why it hasn't been used on an album already. Something about the arrangement, and also the chords in one particular section, makes it reminiscent of 'Even Now', in the most positive sense.

'Days When The Rain Would Come' 4:16

Yet another tune considered for *Like A Rock* but left in the archive, this is one of those bittersweet songs all about the fleeting joys of sunshine. Fogerty had summed up that same feeling aptly in 'Have You Ever Seen The Rain', and Seger captures that same mood in a similarly mid-tempo song – it doesn't last. He has memories of long walks, laughter, discussing closest secrets and eternal happiness. Those were the days when the rain would inevitably come and spoil it all. That excellent, almost rippling piano provides an excellent backbone to it all.

Ultimate Hits: Rock And Roll Never Forgets (2011)

Tracklisting:
Disc 1: 'Old Time Rock And Roll', 'Hollywood Nights', 'Night Moves', 'Main Street', 'Roll Me Away', 'Turn The Page [Live]', 'Her Strut', 'Still The Same', 'You'll Accomp'ny Me', 'We've Got Tonight' [Single Edit], 'Like A Rock', 'Fire Lake', 'Tryin' To Live My Life Without You' [Live]
Disc 2: 'Rock And Roll Never Forgets', 'Against The Wind', 'Ramblin' Gamblin' Man', 'The Fire Down Below', 'Travelin' Man' [Live], 'Beautiful Loser' [Live], 'Shakedown' (Seger, Faltermeyer, Forsey), 'Shame On The Moon (Crowell)', 'Katmandu' [Edited Version], 'The Little Drummer Boy', 'Wait For Me', 'Hey Hey Hey Hey (Going Back To Birmingham)' (Richard Penniman), 'Downtown Train' (Waits)
Walmart exclusive bonus track: 'Living Inside My Heart'
Certification: Platinum (US), Gold (UK)

Artist, management and record company, between them, may have had misgivings about releasing the earlier *Greatest Hits* compilations as doubles on affordability grounds, but at length came up with a 'best of' on two discs.

(The omission of the excellent 'Even Now' from all of these collections was questionable.) This, plus Seger's final two studio albums, *Ride Out* and *I Knew You When*, were issued as usual on Capitol, though this time packaging and CD labels also bore the imprint and logo of Hideout Records & Distributors, Inc., a nod to Andrews' company that had been more or less dormant for some years, alongside the Capitol information.

'Hey Hey Hey Hey (Going Back To Birmingham)' (Richard Penniman) 2:07
One of the vintage rock 'n' roll classics recorded during the same session as the cover of 'Blue Monday', on the *Road House* soundtrack, this was an early Little Richard number from 1955. As usual, his arrangement faithfully follows the original. It's two minutes of sheer musical ecstasy, with Seger working himself up into a frenzy alongside the piano and brass section.

'Downtown Train' (Tom Waits) 3:59
Waits recorded what was to become his most well-known song on *Rain Dogs*, a UK top 30 album in 1985. It received further exposure when Patty Smyth recorded a slightly faster version two years later. In 1989, while on a visit to London, Seger told Rod Stewart he had recorded and was about to release his own take of the song. About a month later, Stewart did likewise and was promptly rewarded with a US number three and UK top ten. A somewhat aggrieved Seger called Stewart 'a non-person' for blatantly copying his idea. Stewart and his management stoutly maintained that his version had already been recorded before both men met. The hatchet was evidently buried when Stewart covered 'Still The Same' for his 2006 album of the same name.

Seger shelved his recording but redid it in 2011 as one of two bonus tracks for *Ultimate Hits*, with Rick Vito adding some gloriously subtle guitar. As a single, it peaked at number 17, his last ever to reach the *Billboard* Adult Contemporary chart.

Unreleased Songs

An article 'Recorded but Unreleased' by Scott Sparling, on the Seger File, the unofficial website, last updated in 2006, lists over 100 songs. Sparling adds that 'based on various statements, it's clear there are hundreds.' Three of them subsequently appeared on the compilation *Early Seger, Vol. 1*. Some are merely listed by title, either with or without the year thought to have been recorded; others have fairly detailed descriptions and quote part of the lyrics.

The majority are Seger's own compositions. One, 'Good Luck Baby Jane', was recorded by Juice Newton and Silver Spur on their album *Come To Me* (1977). Another, 'Long Long Gone', was taped by the writer and his band in Toronto during sessions for *Night Moves*, perhaps one of the four they worked on with Jack Richardson. Although rejected for the album, it was later used by another Detroit outfit, The Rockets, on their album *Turn Up The Radio* (1979). Yet another, 'Hard Night For Sarah', was recorded in 1979 during sessions for *Against The Wind*, but was apparently rejected as it sounded too much like 'Mainstreet'. Kid Rock was later offered it and included it on his eponymous 2003 album.

Another, 'Stranger In Town', was recorded probably in 1977 for the album of the same name. Seger said that a lot of his friends really loved it, but it was very strange. 'It's almost cowboy heavy metal. It's pretty wild. It was actually inspired by the Clint Eastwood spaghetti westerns. It's a very eerie thing, and when I did it, my manager just thought it was way too weird.' In later years, when CDs allowed album reissues to have a capacity for longer playing time and therefore additional tracks, he hoped space might be found for it, but that never came to pass.

Another song that almost but never quite made it several times was, in his words, a 'rather poignant' ballad, 'Can't Hit The Corners No More'. Written as a possible for *Against The Wind*, it was held over for *The Distance*, until he played it to Don Henley, who called it 'a great, great song with a lousy track'. After that, it was to appear on the B-side of 'American Storm'. Seger reportedly pulled it as he was going to offer it to Martin Scorsese for the soundtrack of his forthcoming picture, *The Color Of Money*, but that never happened.

There's plenty to whet the appetite. For example, 'Carfax Abbey' is a song about vampires, the location being a property north of London that Count Dracula bought so he could be near the city and a never-ending supply of fresh blood. The lyrics, however, mislocate the Abbey in the Carpathian Mountains, Eastern Europe. 'The Daughter Was The Mother Of Them All', from 1973, is described as a cross between 'Long Song Comin'' and 'Need Ya', a rocker with a Grimm's fairy tale to the lyrics, or maybe an old English ballad of the kind that Steeleye Span used to adapt. The main characters are a beautiful daughter, a greedy father, a king and some cows with whom the daughter gets too friendly and spoils any chance of marrying the king. 'Elevator Button', his first attempt at reggae, was inspired by the death of

John Belushi, and the kind of person who wants life to be better, faster, 'so they keep pushing these buttons'. It was intended for *The Distance*, but Iovine and Andrews rejected it.

These are only the tip of the iceberg. In 1983, the year after he had released 12 of the 18 studio albums that would appear during his lengthy recording career, he told interviewer Timothy White that he had 100 finished songs recorded, as well as another 400 that were only partly completed. During the 13-year period that he completed four albums, 1982-1995, it was estimated that he had written at least another 120 and recorded at least 90. These albums contained a mere 43 songs, thus leaving a balance of over 50 additional ones recorded, plus about 30 more in demo form.

Several cover versions are mentioned. Apart from The Supremes' 'My World Is Empty Without You' from the *Night Moves* sessions as already noted, they include Fats Domino's 'The Fat Man', Little Richard's 'Keep A'Knockin'', which Seger regularly played live during his early 1970s days with Knape and Teegarden, 'See Me In The Evening', a blues number by Hound Dog Taylor and The HouseRockers, from their 1974 album *Natural Boogie*, The Rolling Stones' classic 'Honky Tonk Women', and the Jackie Wilson evergreen hit, slightly retitled '(Your Love Is Taking Me) Higher And Higher'. There are also two Dylan songs, 'I'll Remember You', intended as the B-side of 'Like A Rock' in 1986, and 'Too Much Of Nothing', which had been considered for *It's A Mystery*, alongside one by Tom Waits, 'Hang Down Your Head'.

Some of these tracks have appeared on two bootleg three-CD sets, *Painting Pictures Of America, Vol. 1* (51 tracks) and *Vol. 2* (54 tracks), both of which contain plenty of demos, outtakes, alternate mixes and live recordings spanning the whole of Seger's career.

He remained as prolific as ever during the final years. About 60 songs were considered but rejected for *Ride Out*, his penultimate album. One, a father-daughter number, 'Hannah', featured guest appearances from Kid Rock and Sheryl Crow.

On the subject of officially releasing archive material, he admitted he had 'some really strange stuff sitting around that might be kind of fun for people to hear after all these years.' Capitol had been talking about it, 'but it would depend on what they would want to put out. What I've got is a lot of outtakes of stuff that I thought were really cool, but things that my manager, Punch, thought were a little too dangerous to put on albums.' Given that Seger's last new album came out in 2017 and he played his last show two years later, few would bet on any of this material being made generally available in the future.

Resources

Books

Balian, E. S., *Turn The Page: The Bob Seger Story* (Silver Sky, 2019)

De Witt, H., & D., *Stranger In Town: The Musical Life Of Del Shannon* (Kendall/Hunt, 2001)

Guterman, J. & O'Donnell, O., *The Worst Rock 'N' Roll Records Of All Time* (Citadel, 1991)

Marsh, D., *Fortunate Son: Criticism And Journalism By America's Best-Known Rock Writer* (Random House, 1985)

Marsh, D., *The Heart Of Rock And Soul* (Da Capo, 1999)

Weschler, T., *Travelin' Man: On The Road And Behind The Scenes With Bob Seger* (Wayne State University Press, 2010)

Articles And Interviews

Freedom Du Lac, J. F., 'It's A Mystery' No More: Seger's Rockin' Again' (*Sacramento Bee*, 14 April 1996)

Graff, G., 'Rocker Tells The Stories Behind The Hits' (*Detroit Free Press*, 18 October 1994)

Hilburn, R., 'Bob Seger, Rock's Prodigal Son' (*Los Angeles Times*, 22 May 1977)

Marsh, D., 'Doncha Ever Listen To The Radio ... How To Remain Obscure Through Better Rock 'N' Roll: Bob Seger, Best In The Midwest' (*Creem*, May 1972)

Morse, S., 'Bob Seger Is Still The Same: The Rock Superstar Stays Close To His Roots' (*Boston Globe*, 14 September 1978)

Morthland, J., 'Bob Seger Conquers The World (And About Time!)' (*Creem*, July 1977)

Pond, S., 'Bob Seger: Nice Guy In The Nasty Lane' (*Rolling Stone*, 3 February 1983)

White, T., 'The Roads Not Taken' (*Musician Player & Listener*, April 1983)

Journals And Newspapers

Billboard

Cash Box

Classic Rock

Detroit Free Press

Los Angeles Times

Melody Maker

Mix

Music Connection

Musician Player & Listener

New Musical Express

New York Times
Record Collector
Rolling Stone
Sounds
USA Today

Internet (accessed November 2025)

Allen, J., 'Noah: The Album That Nearly Ended Bob Seger's Career' (*Rock And Roll Globe*, 5 November 2019)

altrockchick, Bob Seger and the Silver Bullet Band – 'Ultimate Hits: Rock & Roll Never Forgets' (*Classic Music Review,* 11 December 2022)

Corsini, K., 'Bob Seger – 'I Knew You When' (Deluxe) – A Near Miss' (*Classic Rock*, 25 November 2017)

bourbonandvinyl.net

Graff, G., 'Q&A: Bob Seger' (*Classic Rock*, 31 December 2014) *loudersound.com*

Kielty, M., 'Bob Seger's Oceanic Leap For 'The Fire Down Below' (*Classic Rock,* 27 June 2020). *ultimateclassicrock.com*

Kubernik, H., 'A Late '70s Interview With Bob Seger' (*Best Classic Bands*, 6 May 2014) *bestclassicbands.com*

McCollum, B., 'A Definitive Oral History of Seger's Early Years' (*Detroit Free Press*, 14 March 2004) (accessed from Wayback Machine, Internet Archive)

Quirk, T., 'Where Have All The Bob Seger Albums Gone?' (*NPR Music*, 29 March 2017) *npr.org*

Ragogna, M., 'Rock And Roll Never Forgets: An Interview With Bob Seger' (*HuffPost*, 21 November 2011, updated 6 December 2017) *huffpost.com*

Sharp, K., 'How Bob Seger Changed The Face Of American Music' (*Classic Rock,* 10 September 2018) *loudersound.com*

Trakin, R., 'The Creem Interview' (*Creem*, 1 September 1986) *creem.com*

Wheeler, S., 'Bob Seger: End Of An Era' (*Rokritr.com*, 5 November 2019) *rokritr.com*

45cat.com
Allmusic.com
Discogs.com
Segerfile.com
Songfacts.com
Steve Hoffman Music Forums
Vintagerock.com

Also available from Sonicbond

On Track series

AC/DC – Chris Sutton 978-1-78952-307-2
Aerosmith – Andrew Rooney 978-1-78952-364-5
Allman Brothers Band – Andrew Wild 978-1-78952-252-5
Tori Amos – Lisa Torem 978-1-78952-142-9
Aphex Twin – Beau Waddell 978-1-78952-267-9
Asia – Peter Braidis 978-1-78952-099-6
Badfinger – Robert Day-Webb 978-1-878952-176-4
Barclay James Harvest – Keith and Monica Domone 978-1-78952-067-5
Beck – Arthur Lizie 978-1-78952-258-7
The Beat, General Public, Fine Young Cannibals – Steve Parry 978-1-78952-274-7
The Beatles 1962-1996 – Alberto Bravin and Andrew Wild 978-1-78952-355-3
The Beatles Solo 1969-1980 – Andrew Wild 978-1-78952-030-9
Black Sabbath The Dio Years – Chris Sutton 978-1-78952-409-3
Blue Oyster Cult – Jacob Holm-Lupo 978-1-78952-007-1
Blur – Matt Bishop 978-178952-164-1
Marc Bolan and T.Rex – Peter Gallagher 978-1-78952-124-5
David Bowie 1964 to 1982 – Carl Ewens 978-1-78952-324-9
David Bowie 1983 to 2016 – Don Klees 978-1-78952-351-5
Bucks Fizz – David Waterfield 978-1-78952-448-2
Kate Bush – Bill Thomas 978-1-78952-097-2
The Byrds – Andy McArthur 978-1-78952-280-8
Camel – Hamish Kuzminski 978-1-78952-040-8
Captain Beefheart – Opher Goodwin 978-1-78952-235-8
Caravan – Andy Boot 978-1-78952-127-6
Cardiacs – Eric Benac 978-1-78952-131-3
Wendy Carlos – Mark Marrington 978-1-78952-331-7
The Carpenters – Paul Tornbohm 978-1-78952-301-0
Nick Cave and The Bad Seeds – Dominic Sanderson 978-1-78952-240-2
The Chic Organisation – Chris Sutton 97801-78952—366-9
Eric Clapton Solo – Andrew Wild 978-1-78952-141-2
The Clash (revised edition) – Nick Assirati 978-1-78952-325-6
Leonard Cohen – Opher Goodwin 978-1-78952-359-1
Elvis Costello and The Attractions – Georg Purvis 978-1-78952-129-0
Crosby, Stills and Nash – Andrew Wild 978-1-78952-039-2
Creedence Clearwater Revival – Tony Thompson 978-1-78952-237-2
Crowded House – Jon Magidsohn 978-1-78952-292-1
The Cure – Matthew R. Davis 978-1-78952-347-8
The Damned – Morgan Brown 978-1-78952-136-8
Deep Purple and Rainbow 1968-79 (new ed)– Steve Pilkington 978-1-78952-411-6
Deep Purple from 1984 – Phil Kafcaloudes 978-1-78952-354-6
Def Leppard – Scott Robinson 978-1-78952-447-5
Depeche Mode – Brian J. Robb 978-1-78952-277-8
Dire Straits – Andrew Wild 978-1-78952-044-6
The Divine Comedy – Alan Draper 978-1-78952-308-9
The Doobie Brothers – Andrew Wild 978-1-78952-462-8
The Doors – Tony Thompson 978-1-78952-137-5
Dream Theater – Jordan Blum 978-1-78952-050-7
Duran Duran – Karen Windle 978-1-78952-368-3
Ian Dury – Opher Goodwin 978-1-78952-374-4
Bob Dylan 1962-1970 – Opher Goodwin 978-1-78952-275-2
Eagles – John Van der Kiste 978-1-78952-260-0
Earth, Wind and Fire – Bud Wilkins 978-1-78952-272-3
Electric Light Orchestra – Barry Delve 978-1-78952-152-8
Emerson Lake and Palmer – Mike Goode 978-1-78952-000-2
Fairport Convention – Kevan Furbank 978-1-78952-051-4
Focus 1969 to 1985 – Stephen Lambe 978-1-78952-463-5
Peter Gabriel – Graeme Scarfe 978-1-78952-138-2
Genesis – Stuart MacFarlane 978-1-78952-005-7
Gentle Giant – Gary Steel 978-1-78952-058-3
Gong (new edition)– Kevan Furbank 978-1-78952-340-9
Green Day – William E. Spevack 978-1-78952-261-7
Dave Grohl and Foo Fighters – Ben L. Connor 978-1-78952-363-8
Steve Hackett – Geoffrey Feakes 978-1-78952-098-9
Hall and Oates – Ian Abrahams 978-1-78952-167-2
Peter Hammill – Richard Rees Jones 978-1-78952-163-4

Roy Harper – Opher Goodwin 978-1-78952-130-6
Hawkwind (new edition) – Duncan Harris 978-1-78952-290-7
Jimi Hendrix – Emma Stott 978-1-78952-175-7
The Hollies – Andrew Darlington 978-1-78952-159-7
Horslips – Richard James 978-1-78952-263-1
The Human League and The Sheffield Scene – Andrew Darlington 978-1-78952-186-3
Humble Pie –Robert Day-Webb 978-1-78952-2761
Ian Hunter – G. Mick Smith 978-1-78952-304-1
Iggy and the Stooges – Robert Day-Webb 978-1-78952-360-7
Iggy Pop 1977 to 1999 – Hans Meertens 978-1-78952-446-8
The Incredible String Band – Tim Moon 978-1-78952-107-8
INXS – Manny Grillo 978-1-78952-302-7
Iron Maiden (new ed) – Steve Pilkington 978-1-78952-380-5
Joe Jackson – Richard James 978-1-78952-189-4
The Jam – Stan Jeffries 978-1-78952-299-0
Jefferson Airplane – Richard Butterworth 978-1-78952-143-6
Jethro Tull – Jordan Blum 978-1-78952-016-3
J. Geils Band – James Romag 978-1-78952-332-4
Elton John in the 1970s – Peter Kearns 978-1-78952-034-7
Billy Joel – Lisa Torem 978-1-78952-183-2
Journey – Doug Thornton 978-1-78952-337-9
Judas Priest – John Tucker 978-1-78952-018-7
Killing Joke – Nic Ransome 978-1-78952-273-0
The Kinks – Martin Hutchinson 978-1-78952-172-6
Korn – Matt Karpe 978-1-78952-153-5
Led Zeppelin – Steve Pilkington 978-1-78952-151-1
Level 42 – Matt Philips 978-1-78952-102-3
Little Feat – Georg Purvis 978-1-78952-168-9
Lynyrd Skynyrd – Chris Salisbury 978-1-78952-472-7
Love – Emma Stott 978-1-78952-4642
Magnum – Matthew Taylor 978-1-78952-286-0
Aimee Mann – Jez Rowden 978-1-78952-036-1
MC5 – Richard Butterworth 978-1-78952-377-5
Ralph McTell – Paul O. Jenkins 978-1-78952-294-5
Metallica – Barry Wood 978-1-78952-269-3
Joni Mitchell – Peter Kearns 978-1-78952-081-1
The Moody Blues – Geoffrey Feakes 978-1-78952-042-2
Motorhead – Duncan Harris 978-1-78952-173-3
Nektar – Scott Meze 978-1-78952-257-0
New Order – Dennis Remmer 978-1-78952-249-5
Nightwish – Simon McMurdo 978-1-78952-270-9
Nirvana – William E. Spevack 978-1-78952-318-8
Laura Nyro – Philip Ward 978-1-78952-182-5
Oasis – Andrew Rooney 978-1-78952-300-3
Phil Ochs – Opher Goodwin 978-1-78952-326-3
Mike Oldfield – Ryan Yard 978-1-78952-060-6
Opeth – Jordan Blum 978-1-78-952-166-5
Pearl Jam – Ben L. Connor 978-1-78952-188-7
Tom Petty – Richard James 978-1-78952-128-3
Anthony Phillips – Alan Draper 978-1-78952-356-0
Pink Floyd – Richard Butterworth 978-1-78952-242-6
The Police – Pete Braidis 978-1-78952-158-0
The Pretenders 1978 to 1990 Richard Butterworth 978-1-78952-358-4
Porcupine Tree (Revised Edition) – Nick Holmes 978-1-78952-346-1
Procol Harum – Scott Meze 978-1-78952-315-7
Queen – Andrew Wild 978-1-78952-003-3
Radiohead – William Allen 978-1-78952-149-8
Gerry Rafferty – John Van der Kiste 978-1-78952-349-2
Rancid – Paul Matts 978-1-78952-187-0
Lou Reed 1972-1986 – Ethan Roy 978-1-78952-283-9
Renaissance – David Detmer 978-1-78952-062-0
REO Speedwagon – Jim Romag 978-1-78952-262-4
The Rolling Stones 1963-80 – Steve Pilkington 978-1-78952-017-0
Linda Ronstadt 1969-1989 – Daryl O. Lawrence 987-1-78952-293-8
Roxy Music – Michael Kulikowski 978-1-78952-335-5
Rush 1973 to 1982 – Richard James 978-1-78952-338-6

Rush 1984 to 2015 - Richard James 978-1-78952-372-0
Sensational Alex Harvey Band – Peter Gallagher 978-1-7952-289-1
The Small Faces and The Faces – Andrew Darlington 978-1-78952-316-4
The Smashing Pumpkins – Matt Karpe 978-1-7952-291-4
The Smiths and Morrissey – Tommy Gunnarsson 978-1-78952-140-5
Soft Machine – Scott Meze 978-1078952-271-6
Sparks 1969-1979 – Chris Sutton 978-1-78952-279-2
Spirit – Rev. Keith A. Gordon 978-1-78952- 248-8
Bruce Springsteen - David Starkey 978-1-78952-471-0
Stackridge – Alan Draper 978-1-78952-232-7
Status Quo the Frantic Four Years – Richard James 978-1-78952-160-3
Steeleye Span 1970-1989 – Darren Johnson 989-1-78952-369-0
Steely Dan – Jez Rowden 978-1-78952-043-9
The Stranglers – Martin Hutchinson 978-1-78952-323-2
Talk Talk – Gary Steel 978-1-78952-284-6
Talking Heads – David Starkey 978-178952-353-9
Tears For Fears – Paul Clark 978-178952-238-9
The Temptations 1960 to 1978 – George Haffenden 978-178952-373-7
The The –Brian J. Robb 978-178952-370-6
Thin Lizzy – Graeme Stroud 978-1-78952-064-4
Tool – Matt Karpe 978-1-78952-234-1
Toto – Jacob Holm-Lupo 978-1-78952-019-4
U2 – Eoghan Lyng 978-1-78952-078-1
UFO – Richard James 978-1-78952-073-6
Ultravox – Brian J. Robb 978-1-78952-330-0
Van Der Graaf Generator – Dan Coffey 978-1-78952-031-6
Van Halen – Morgan Brown 9781-78952-256-3
Suzanne Vega – Lisa Torem 978-1-78952-281-5
Jack White And The White Stripes – Ben L. Connor 978-1-78952-303-4
The Who – Geoffrey Feakes 978-1-78952-076-7
Steven Wilson – Insurgentes-To The Bone – Nick Holmes 978-1-78952-317-1
Wishbone Ash 1970 to 1982 978-1-78952-413-0
Roy Wood and the Move – James R Turner 978-1-78952-008-8
The Yardbirds – Andrew Darlington 978-1-78952-362-1
Yes (new edition) – Stephen Lambe 978-1-78952-282-2
Neil Young 1963 to 1970 – Oper Goodwin 978-1-78952-298-3
Frank Zappa 1966 to 1979 – Eric Benac 978-1-78952-033-0
Warren Zevon – Peter Gallagher 978-1-78952-170-2
The Zombies – Emma Stott 978-1-78952-297-6
10CC – Peter Kearns 978-1-78952-054-5

Decades Series

The Bee Gees in the 1960s – Andrew Mon Hughes et al 978-1-78952-148-1
The Bee Gees in the 1970s – Andrew Mon Hughes et al 978-1-78952-179-5
The Bee Gees in the 1980s – Andrew Mon Hughes et al 978-1-78952-497-0
Black Sabbath in the 1970s – Chris Sutton 978-1-78952-171-9
Britpop – Peter Richard Adams and Matt Pooler 978-1-78952-169-6
Phil Collins in the 1980s – Andrew Wild 978-1-78952-185-6
Alice Cooper in the 1970s – Chris Sutton 978-1-78952-104-7
Alice Cooper in the 1980s – Chris Sutton 978-1-78952-259-4
Curved Air in the 1970s – Laura Shenton 978-1-78952-069-9
Donovan in the 1960s – Jeff Fitzgerald 978-1-78952-233-4
Bob Dylan in the 1980s – Don Klees 978-1-78952-157-3
Brian Eno in the 1970s – Gary Parsons 978-1-78952-239-6
Faith No More in the 1990s – Matt Karpe 978-1-78952-250-1
Fleetwood Mac in the 1970s – Andrew Wild 978-1-78952-105-4
Fleetwood Mac in the 1980s – Don Klees 978-178952-254-9
Focus in the 1970s – Stephen Lambe 978-1-78952-079-8
Free and Bad Company in the 1970s – John Van der Kiste 978-1-78952-178-8
Genesis in the 1970s – Bill Thomas 978178952-146-7
George Harrison in the 1970s – Eoghan Lyng 978-1-78952-174-0
Kiss in the 1970s – Peter Gallagher 978-1-78952-246-4
Manfred Mann's Earth Band in the 1970s – John Van der Kiste 978178952-243-3
Marillion in the 1980s – Nathaniel Webb 978-1-78952-065-1
Van Morrison in the 1970s – Peter Childs 978-1-78952-241-9
Mott the Hoople & Ian Hunter in the 1970s – John Van der Kiste 978-1-78-952-162-7
Pink Floyd In The 1970s – Georg Purvis 978-1-78952-072-9

Suzi Quatro in the 1970s – Darren Johnson 978-1-78952-236-5
Queen in the 1970s – James Griffiths 978-1-78952-265-5
Roxy Music in the 1970s – Dave Thompson 978-1-78952-180-1
Slade in the 1970s – Darren Johnson 978-1-78952-268-6
Status Quo in the 1980s – Greg Harper 978-1-78952-244-0
The Sweet in the 1970s – Darren Johnson 978-1-78952-139-9
Uriah Heep in the 1970s – Steve Pilkington 978-1-78952-103-0
Van der Graaf Generator in the 1970s – Steve Pilkington 978-1-78952-245-7
Rick Wakeman in the 1970s – Geoffrey Feakes 978-1-78952-264-8
Yes in the 1980s – Stephen Lambe with David Watkinson 978-1-78952-125-2

Rock Classics Series

90125 by Yes – Stephen Lambe 978-1-78952-329-4
Bat Out Of Hell by Meatloaf – Geoffrey Feakes 978-1-78952-320-1
Bringing It All Back Home by Bob Dylan – Opher Goodwin 978-1-78952-314-0
Californication by Red Hot Chili Peppers - Matt Karpe 978-1-78952-348-5
Crime Of The Century by Supertramp – Steve Pilkington 978-1-78952-327-0
The Dreaming by Kate Bush – Peter Kearns 978-1-78952-341-6
Let It Bleed by The Rolling Stones – John Van der Kiste 978-1-78952-309-6
Purple Rain by Prince – Matt Karpe 978-1-78952-322-5
The White Album by The Beatles – Opher Goodwin 978-1-78952-333-1

On Screen Series

Carry On... – Stephen Lambe 978-1-78952-004-0
David Cronenberg – Patrick Chapman 978-1-78952-071-2
Doctor Who: The David Tennant Years – Jamie Hailstone 978-1-78952-066-8
James Bond – Andrew Wild 978-1-78952-010-1
Monty Python – Steve Pilkington 978-1-78952-047-7
Seinfeld Seasons 1 to 5 – Stephen Lambe 978-1-78952-012-5

Other Books

1967: A Year In Psychedelic Rock – Kevan Furbank 978-1-78952-155-9
1970: A Year In Rock – John Van der Kiste 978-1-78952-147-4
1972: The Year Progressive Rock Ruled The World – Kevan Furbank 978-1-78952-288-4
1973: The Golden Year of Progressive Rock – Geoffrey Feakes - 978-1-78952-165-8
1974: The Year Progressive Rock Came Of Age – Kevan Furbank 978-1-78952-473-4
1977: How Progressive Rock Defied Punk – Kevan Furbank - 978-1-78952-367-6
Apple Of My Eye: The Story Of Apple Records – Andrew Wild 978-1-78952-379-9
Eric Clapton Sessions – Andrew Wild 978-1-78952-177-1
Constellation Heroes – Hans Meertens 978-1-78952-498-7
Dark Horse Records – Aaron Badgley 978-1-78952-287-7
Derek Taylor: For Your Radioactive Children – Andrew Darlington 978-1-78952-038-5
Ghosts – Journeys To Post-Pop – Matthew Restall 978-1-78952-334-8
The Golden Age of Easy Listening – Derek Taylor 978-1-78952-285-3
The Golden Road: The Recording History of The Grateful Dead – John Kilbride 978-1-78952-156-6
Hoggin' The Page – Groudhogs The Classic Years – Martyn Hanson 978-1-78952-343-0
Iggy and The Stooges On Stage 1967-1974 – Per Nilsen 978-1-78952-101-6
Jon Anderson and the Warriors – the Road to Yes – David Watkinson 978-1-78952-059-0
Magic: The David Paton Story – David Paton 978-1-78952-266-2
Misty: The Music of Johnny Mathis – Jakob Baekgaard 978-1-78952-247-1
Music in the 1980s – Peter Woolliscoft 978-1-78952-347-8
Nu Metal: A Definitive Guide – Matt Karpe 978-1-78952-063-7
Phish- Baker's Dozen – Brent Waltz 978-1-78952-361-4
Philip Lynott – Renegade – Alan Byrne 978-1-78952-339-3
Remembering Live Aid – Andrew Wild 978-1-78952-328-7
Thank You For The Days – Fans Of The Kinks Share 60 Years of Stories – Ed. Chris Kocher 978-1-78952-342-3
The Making Of Abba – Joe Matera -978-178952-378-2
The Sonicbond On Track Sampler 978-1-78952-190-0
The Sonicbond Progressive Rock Sampler (Ebook only) 978-1-78952-056-9
Tommy Bolin: In and Out of Deep Purple – Laura Shenton 978-1-78952-070-5
Maximum Darkness – Deke Leonard 978-1-78952-048-4
The Twang Dynasty – Deke Leonard 978-1-78952-049-1
Van der Graaf Generator – Pawn Hearts – Paolo Carnelli 978-1-78952-357-7

... and many more to come!

Would you like to write for Sonicbond Publishing?

We are mainly a music publisher, but we also occasionally publish in other genres including film and television. At Sonicbond Publishing we are always on the look-out for authors, particularly for our two main series, On Track and Decades.

Mixing fact with in depth analysis, the On Track series examines the entire recorded work of a particular musical artist or group. All genres are considered from easy listening and jazz to 60s soul to 90s pop, via rock and metal.

The Decades series singles out a particular decade in an artist or group's history and focuses on that decade in more detail than may be allowed in the On Track series.

While professional writing experience would, of course, be an advantage, the most important qualification is to have real enthusiasm and knowledge of your subject. First-time authors are welcomed, but the ability to write well in English is essential.

Sonicbond Publishing has distribution throughout Europe and North America, and all our books are also published in E-book form. Authors will be paid a royalty based on sales of their book. Further details about our books are available from www.sonicbondpublishing.com. To contact us, complete the contact form there or email info@sonicbondpublishing.co.uk